Woven in the Wake of Grief

Frankie Kounouho

Foreword

In the fabric of life, some threads weave together experiences of profound loss and unexpected grace. In this deeply heartfelt narrative, the author bravely shares their journey through the devastating loss of their son, Donovin. This book is more than just an account of grief; it is a testament to the resilience of the human spirit and the transformative power of faith.

As we turn these pages, we are invited into an intimate exploration of sorrow, hope, and the relentless search for meaning in the face of tragedy. The author's raw honesty and vulnerability illuminate the darkest corners of despair, while their quest for connection with God unfolds a path of healing that will resonate with many. It is a journey that speaks to the heart, offering both comfort and encouragement to anyone walking through their own struggles.

In a world that often struggles to understand the depth of such loss, this story shines as a beacon of light, guiding us toward understanding, compassion, and ultimately, redemption. The road to healing is not easy, but it is filled with moments of grace that remind us of the enduring love that remains—even in the absence of those we hold dear.

May this book offer solace to those who grieve and inspire all of us to seek the divine in our struggles. It serves as a powerful reminder that, even in our darkest hours, we are never truly alone on this journey.

— Frankie Kounouho

Dedication

To my beloved son, Donovin Malachi Stokes—thank you for showing me the true meaning of unconditional love. It has been the greatest honor of my life to be your mother.

Acknowledgments

First and foremost, I give my deepest thanks to my Heavenly Father, whose grace, mercy, and love brought me low only to raise me up again.

To Donovin's father, Malachi Stokes—though you left this life before him, I take comfort knowing you were there to welcome him into heaven.

To my mother, Sheryl Davis-Bryant, your unwavering support has been my strength through every storm. I love you beyond words, and I know Doni loved and cherished his Nana.

To my brother, Danin Bryant, who left us before this book was finished—your strength during my darkest moments filled a void I could not have faced alone.

To my dad, Russell Bryant, thank you for being a pillar of support. Doni love and adored his Pop Pop.

To my sister, Stacey Bryant, thank you for your love and encouragement to follow my dreams.

To my father, Jerry Sanders, I'm deeply moved by the tribute you wrote for your grandson. I am forever grateful that you got to meet Donovin.

To my sister, Janeen Sanders, your presence during this time has meant more to me than you'll ever know.

To my dear friend, Gail Washington, thank you for bringing me joy when I felt lost and for opening your home as a refuge for me to find peace and rest.

To my cherished friend, LaMetra Atkins, who left this world too soon—I hope you and Donovin are sharing laughter in heaven, just as you did here on earth.

To Judge Rachel Carrillo, Lisa Carrillo, Jory Plotts, Sandy Spoon, CeCe Mada, Vic and Vera Jones—your support and love on that heart-wrenching day means more to me than words can express.

To my best friend, Lisa Stanton, thank you for always being there to listen without judgement and for your unwavering love and support.

To my forever friend, Wayne Hightower, Jr., thank you for being the one to provide an ear and laughter when I needed it most.

To my beloved sister/friend, Laura Mathieux, thank you for gently encouraging me to finish this book and walk and live this purposeful life.

To my dear friend, Carol Risch, words will never be available to express my gratitude for you during the most difficult season of my life. Thank you for allowing me to go through the grieving process as I needed to.

To my squad—Maureen McQueen-Eller, Alyson Simonds, and Angie Jordan—thank you for your love and encouragement as I navigated life after Donovin's transition. Now go hold that plank for 8, 7, 6, 4, 3, 5, 4, 3, 2, 1 (Laura's counting!)

To my dear Heather Aroesty, your grounding presence has been invaluable. Thank you for always cheering me on and encouraging me to be bold, kick fear in the face, and achieve a great yogi squat.

To my extended family and friends, your life-giving words through sorrow and joy have been a blessing. I am grateful to each of you.

Lastly, but absolutely not lease, to my wonderful husband, Hilaire M. Kounouho—thank you for helping me rediscover laughter, love, and the beauty of life. Thank you for walking this journey called life with me and for cultivating an even more beautiful relationship with God through our marriage. You mean the world to me.

Contents

Introduction

Four years with someone can feel like a lifetime. In that time, we gather moments and memories that shape and often change us in ways we never anticipated. There are moments so full of joy that you wish you could capture them forever—not just in your mind but in photos you could share with friends, family, and even strangers, hoping they could feel the same joy you do in that perfect moment. Yet, there are also moments you wish you could erase—memories of pain and heartache that tear at your soul. You long to forget those moments, but life doesn't work that way. Our memories, both beautiful and painful, are part of our journey.

We are meant to feel, to remember, and to endure—even when the moments feel unbearable. The truth is, we cannot escape our memories. But how we choose to face them—whether we let them destroy us or allow them to heal and strengthen us—shapes who we become. The choice is ours: to sink into despair or rise above it, growing stronger in the face of pain

.

For me, those four years changed everything. I lost track of how many times I said, "I'll do it tomorrow." Taking that dream trip, reconnecting with old friends, visiting family, or telling the people I love how much I care—these were all things I postponed, believing I had endless tomorrows. But when those four years ended, I faced a harsh truth: tomorrow had run out. The moments I let slip away were gone forever.

It was in the sterile, cold hallway of the hospital that the weight of that truth hit me. As I stood there, waiting to enter a room where life as I knew it would shatter, it felt like all the air had been sucked from the room. There was no escape from the news I had just received. It was either swallowing the harsh reality, enduring the painful grief that would follow, or choking on it, which would undoubtedly destroy me. I had to make a choice—one that would determine whether I sank deeper into darkness or found a way to survive.

This is the story of how I made that choice, found my way through the darkest days of my life, and experienced transformation through my relationship with God. From the depths of pain, depression, and suicidal thoughts, I began a journey toward healing, purpose, peace, and praise. It wasn't easy, but every step was worth it.

Chapter One

The Unexpected Diagnosis

What kind of doctor are you? That was the first thought that popped into my head as I studied the man standing before me. Towering tall with dark hair and hazel eyes, he looked as polished as a mannequin in a luxury storefront. His pristine white lab coat contrasted sharply with a multicolored tie featuring bizarre, mismatched animals—a purple giraffe and a green monkey, the likes of which I'd never seen in nature. Pediatrician, maybe? That might explain the whimsical tie. His tailored grey slacks, neatly cuffed at the ankles, and shiny black dress shoes gave him an air of meticulous precision, as if he'd just stepped out of a fashion catalog.

His slightly tanned complexion hinted at just enough time in the sun without overdoing it. Every detail of his grooming was impeccable—clean-shaven, nails precisely trimmed, and an overall polished appearance. The only imperfection? His scent—or lack thereof—which seemed intentional. As a doctor, it made sense to prioritize neutrality over extravagance.

As my internal critique continued, I wondered: Could I really trust this man with my health? Was he just a doctor obsessed with appearances, or did he genuinely know his stuff? His soft, monotone voice, almost therapeutic in its cadence, only added to the mystery. "Dr. Patterson," he said, introducing himself as my new primary care physician.

Without warning, he launched into a barrage of health-related questions, his delivery so rehearsed it felt like he was reading from a script. I answered politely—at least outwardly. In my head, though, I was already roasting him. "What brings you in today?" he asked, his tone clinical.

"Well, doc," I thought sarcastically, "I've been feeling a little under the weather. Maybe it's a cold. Maybe the flu."

The exam was routine—blood work, a urine sample, the usual checklist. Before leaving, he paused and asked, "Is it possible that you're pregnant?" His tone carried an air of certainty, as if he already knew the answer.

Inwardly, I scoffed, "Of course it's possible. I'm married, and last I checked, marriage comes with certain liberties." At the mention of pregnancy, I shot a quick glance at Malachi. He sat up straight in his chair, suddenly alert, his expression betraying a mix of surprise and curiosity.

My internal monologue was on fire. "Doctor Fancy Pants, if you can't figure out that I just have the flu, maybe I need to find a new doctor," I thought, imagining myself with my hands on my hips and giving him a disapproving look.

But outwardly, I responded, ever so gently, "Yes,

doctor, I could be pregnant."

As Dr. Patterson stepped out to confirm my diagnosis, doubt crept in. Could I really trust him? The room felt cold, and I reclined on the exam table, the smooth jazz playing softly in the background lulling me into a light doze. A sudden crash—Malachi knocking over a box of tissues—jolted me back to reality.

His look, when he turned to face me, was almost knowing. As if he'd somehow read my mind. I wasn't sure if he was annoyed or exhilarated by the opportunity to prove himself right. But when he handed me the results—"you are pregnant," it was like the floor dropped out from under me.

For a moment, I stared at the paper in disbelief. I wanted to will the word "POSITIVE" to disappear. Maybe this was someone else's test result? No. It was mine.

My internal dialogue continued. "You sneaky little bastard, you knew all along, didn't you? You just asked me to confirm it, didn't you?" I glanced up at Dr. Patterson, half-expecting to see some sign that he could hear my thoughts. He looked down at my chart as if he hadn't heard a thing—but then quickly glanced back at me.

For a second, I entertained the possibility that Dr. Fancy Pants could read minds. The idea was absurd, but for a brief moment, I thought maybe he was toying with me. I quickly dismissed it. No way. I was just overthinking things.

Dr. Patterson shifted on his feet, still holding my test results like a prized possession. His expression hadn't changed, but there was something in his eyes that I couldn't place. It was too... calm. He wasn't reacting the way I expected. Most doctors would at least show a hint of surprise or concern when delivering unexpected news, but not him. He just stood there, waiting for my reaction.

I blinked a few times, still trying to process. The room felt like it was spinning now, as though the walls themselves were closing in. Was this really happening? Was I really pregnant? But I'd only just found out I was late. How could this be?

Malachi, ever the observer, had been quiet the entire time, but now he stood up from his seat, his face a mixture of concern and disbelief. I could see his mind working, trying to piece together what this meant, just like me. But there was no avoiding it. This was real.

I took a deep breath, trying to steady my racing thoughts. "What do we do now?" I asked, my voice trembling. The question sounded weak to my own ears, but it was the only one I could think of at that moment.

Dr. Patterson's eyes finally softened, and he set the results down on the counter before taking a step closer. "Now, we start discussing your options," he said, his tone still measured but no longer impassive. "But first, I think we should talk about how you're feeling. Physically, emotionally..."

I swallowed hard, trying to gather my thoughts. The words were all blending together. Emotionally? Was he really asking about my emotions? Wasn't this supposed to be about my health? But before I could respond, he added, "It's a big change, and I want you to feel supported."

Support. That word felt foreign to me in that moment. Support? Was I even ready for this? Would Malachi and I be okay? The questions raced through my mind faster than I could process them, but I nodded slowly. I had no idea what the next step was, but I knew I had to start somewhere.

As Dr. Patterson began outlining a few basic steps for follow-up care and what to expect in the coming weeks, my mind wandered again. This moment felt surreal—like I was watching myself from the outside, detached, as if this was happening to someone else entirely. But no, it was me. And now, I had to figure out how to deal with it. How to wrap my head around the fact that my life was about to change in ways I couldn't even begin to imagine.

And yet, through it all, Dr. Patterson remained calm, steady, almost... reassuring. It was hard to decide whether I felt comforted or unsettled by his unwavering composure.

Chapter Two

The Church

On the drive home from the doctor's office, the silence between Malachi and me was deafening. My mind raced with questions, and I think I could even hear his. A million thoughts flooded my mind in an instant: *Will the baby be a boy or a girl? What will we do with a baby? I wonder what he or she will look like. Wait—did the doctor actually say the pregnancy test was positive? What exactly does that mean? Could it be one of those false positives they talk about on TV? Would we be good parents?*

Then the realization hit me like a wave, and tears began to flow—not the ugly, heaving kind, but a quiet, solemn cry. This baby, at some point, would have to come out of me. How had I overlooked such a monumental detail? Whether through a vaginal birth or a C-section, this child would need to leave the sanctuary where it had been growing for weeks.

As we drove quietly down Peachtree Street, my mind kept circling around one thought: this baby was going to have to come out eventually. Neither of us said a word. We just sat there, lost in our own thoughts, staring blankly through the windshield. My mind, however, was a swirling mess of imagined scenarios about childbirth. I started playing a silent game of *"I'd Rather!"*—a game where you list a few things you'd rather do than the thing you *have* to do. My game began with, *I'd rather get a root canal with mild anesthesia than have to let a baby pass through my birth canal.*

I played the game for a while, each new "I'd rather" becoming more absurd than the last. Occasionally, I giggled to myself, and Malachi would blink but never turn toward me or react. Was he playing his own version of *"I'd Rather"* in his head? I wondered if the excitement was slipping away for him too.

When my game ended, I turned inward, silently calling on the Lord. Isn't that what most of us do in moments of fear or uncertainty? Even those who rarely set foot in a church—or don't believe at all—seem to call out in times of crisis. I thought about the millions of prayers offered daily by people everywhere: the devout, the doubters, and those simply seeking solace in a moment of panic.

I reflected on my relationship with God. As a child, Sunday School meant singing songs about Jesus and feeling God's love. It always seemed personal, like those songs were written just for me. But as I grew older, I drifted away. I moved further from God, though I never felt He had moved far from me. I just couldn't pinpoint what was missing.

I occasionally visited random churches, though I couldn't quite explain why. Maybe I thought that something, someone, would give me the answers I was searching for. I knew I wasn't looking in vain, but I never seemed to find what I needed.

Was God even listening to my cries for help now, in this moment of fear and uncertainty about giving birth? After all, I had been unfaithful to the church, flitting from one congregation to another without ever truly committing. It seemed like I was cheating on God, too, by not fully investing in any one community. And yet, somewhere deep down, I knew I wasn't alone in that feeling.

I had come to understand that the church itself had also failed me. The building, the programs, the people—they never encouraged or helped cultivate my relationship with God. It was like we were both cheating on each other, and I had begun to accept that it was up to me to fill the void. But where was I supposed to go for help? Where were the knowledgeable, experienced individuals who could guide me?

Throughout my life, I had been longing to find something more. I believed that somehow, I would find it in God, in the church, but the answers never seemed to come. I wanted to understand Him, know Him, feel His presence, but it was as if He were hiding from me.

Now, here I was again, stepping into another church, hopeful for change yet anticipating disappointment. My experiences in churches spanned the spectrum—from deeply disheartening to fleeting moments of connection that left me yearning for more. Each departure only amplified the distance I felt from God.

I remembered one church experience in particular, one that made me label this particular place the *"Pimp House Church."* I was young, single, and eager to find God, not a date. But some of the male churchgoers had other ideas. I never expected to find myself in a situation where the church, a supposed sanctuary, became a breeding ground for unwanted advances.

The Pimp House Church was a small congregation of about seventy, where women greatly outnumbered the men. Located in a dilapidated warehouse in an industrial part of the city, the setting lacked any sense of sacredness. Concrete floors, metal folding chairs, and a DIY wooden cross adorned with plastic jewels and artificial flowers gave the space an oddly makeshift quality—hardly what one would expect in a house of God.

It was my second visit to this church. I had been invited back after my first visit, which was rather unassuming, but the invitation came with a twist: I should return to receive *"The Word."* I wasn't sure what I received the first time, but clearly, with the second invitation, I decided to give it another chance.

In my younger years, I was fit, healthy, and attractive— some might even say beautiful. I took pride in my appearance and felt confident in how I looked, knowing that my physical fitness was a reflection of the effort I put into staying active and taking care of myself. As the years went by, my appearance naturally evolved, but the essence of my beauty remained unchanged. This isn't about vanity—just a reflection on how time shapes us all. Let's just say that gravity made a bra a more essential part of my wardrobe.

But at that moment, I was young and, in some ways, naive, walking into what felt like a den of lions. I would later be thankful that I wasn't in that den alone—God was with me, even if I didn't realize it at the time.

The first male encounter was, well, rather corny. This guy's approach was to ask if I'd like to "bible-study" with him at his home on a Friday night—just the two of us, around 8:00 that evening. Apparently, he was "more coherent" in the evening than the morning or afternoon, and clearly more "God-like" at his home. Needless to say, our *"bible-study"* session didn't happen—not because I didn't want to study, but because I didn't feel safe with the time or location, not to mention this poor guy had a severe case of halitosis.

There was no way around it. I politely let him know that *"bible-study"* in his home on a Friday night was not going to happen and with even more politeness, I let him know about his breath issue, and needless to say, he never spoke to me again.

At this same church, four other men approached me, two of whom were married, each with different propositions. One asked me to have dinner, another invited me to a movie, and two were blunt enough to suggest that we "get together" in a more intimate way. All of them assured me that *The Word* of God would be discussed—though, I'm sure their version of discussing God wasn't what I nor God had in mind. None of the invitations were accepted and my search for God only seemed more complicated. I was determined, I was there for one reason: I was on a mission to find God. Entertaining any of these men would only take me further away from that goal.

I should mention that I brought all of these concerns to the pastor and his wife on my second (and final) visit to this church. To my disappointment, they weren't surprised. They knew what was going on but chose to turn a blind eye. Was this the will of God? Was God even paying attention to the dysfunction happening under His name? That day, I didn't get any answers, but I would eventually.

Several months and many churches later, a friend of mine—who I had once considered a true friend—invited me to her church. Surprisingly, I was willing to give God and His people another chance. Maybe this time I would find Him. Maybe this time, He wouldn't just be an image on a cross or a figure in a painting. Maybe He was real, and just maybe, He had something to show me.

By this point, this was probably my tenth visit to some church or another, but my internal longing for God seemed to grow louder and more elusive with each passing year. I couldn't shake the feeling that I needed something bigger than myself.

My friend gave me the details for the church—name, address, and time—and I was eager to try again. I arrived about fifteen minutes early and immediately noticed the parking lot was full. *Wow*, this had to be a good sign, right? Maybe this time, God and I would finally meet.

I still remember the ankle-length brown linen summer dress I wore that warm morning. I picked it deliberately because it was modest, covering every inch of my body to avoid giving any church lady the wrong impression—that I had just left my job on a pole or was seeking male attention.

It reminded me of the time I wore a skirt that draped just past my knees at another church, only to be told by a stranger (a church lady, of course) that I needed to cover my legs. When I questioned her, citing Christ's words that I should come as I am, she snapped back. She told me that at her church, my attire wasn't acceptable, and I needed to cover my legs or leave. So, I left.

But here I was again, walking into this church, wearing my long brown dress, arms covered, and a slip underneath to ensure nothing would be revealed if the light hit me the wrong way. I hoped I would be accepted, that I would find a place where I could simply be.

A middle-aged woman greeted me immediately as I approached the doors. She asked who I was and what brought me there. I answered as best I could, but her last question threw me off. *What brought you here?* It's a church, isn't it obvious? Like going to a restaurant, there's a clear reason for being there: to receive food. So, I responded honestly, "I'm Frankie, and I'm hoping to meet God here."

Her reaction surprised me. She looked at me, confused, before silently pointing toward the double doors. Was this a red flag? Maybe she knew I wouldn't find God here after all. Maybe she was surprised by my honesty.

I stood there for a moment, pondering whether I should be scared, but in the end, I entered the double doors, hoping that this wouldn't be my downfall.

The church itself was a small building that resembled an old schoolhouse from the pioneer days, nestled in a clearing in the woods. The white paint had faded, and the bell tower at the top looked like something from the Salem witch trials era. I half wondered if the bell still worked—or if it did, how they would ring it without knocking the tower over.

I didn't have much time to wonder, though, as I walked inside and was immediately struck by the contrast between the building's old exterior and the modern interior. The entryway was a soft grey carpet that led into the sanctuary, where beautiful multi-colored tiles covered the floor. The pews were a deep wine color, complementing the tiles and the altar, which I could see from the back of the room. It was a striking sight—an altar that looked as though God Himself had designed it.

Before I could fully absorb the beauty of the space, I felt a warm hand on my right arm and an embrace around my waist. My friend had arrived and was happy to see me, pulling me closer for a hug. I smiled, my heart filled with excitement. *Maybe, just maybe*, I thought, *this is where I'll meet God.*

She directed me to a seat, and as I settled in, I noticed the man next to me. He was dressed impeccably in his Sunday best, and he smiled warmly at me as I caught his gaze. I returned the smile and greeted him. This time, there was a sense of calm in me. Maybe this place was different.

The church was packed—well, for this church, that meant about eighty-five to one hundred people. I was mesmerized by all the colorful clothing the people were wearing. When the singing started, I stood up, swaying to the music, even changing the lyrics from time to time since I didn't know the songs, but I enjoyed the tune. I was having a good time, looking around at the smiling, happy faces greeting me.

When the singing ended, the pastor approached the podium and shouted, *"Thank You, Jesus! Thank You for this glorious day and for the people of this house."* Instinctively, I clapped along with everyone else, feeling the excitement building.

When he instructed the congregation to take their seats, I quickly sat down, eagerly anticipating that at any moment, I would finally meet God.

The pastor began speaking, reading from Matthew 11:28-30. Don't worry—I had to grab a Bible from the shelf behind the pew in front of me to follow along. It was a familiar verse:

"Come to me, all you who are weary and burdened, and I will give you rest. Take my yoke upon you and learn from me, for I am gentle and humble in heart, and you will find rest for your souls."

YES. I felt a surge of excitement. This was it! The pastor clearly knew why I was there. God must know, too. Why else would he start with this verse? My anticipation was overflowing. This was exactly what I needed to hear.

I listened intently as the pastor read aloud and then offered his commentary. Everything seemed to make sense: if I came to God, He would give me calmness and rest from the struggles of everyday life. This was the path to building a solid relationship with God. Surely, I needed rest and peace, and if building a relationship with God required certain steps, I was ready to take them.

The words felt right, and even the pastor's commentary seemed to align with what I needed to hear. But just as quickly as I thought God had met me there, it felt like He—and I— were being swept away.

My sudden shift in emotions came when the pastor began calling people from the pews to the altar. One by one, he pointed to individuals, and they walked up, where he laid his hand on their foreheads. The congregation erupted in shouting, screaming, and speaking in tongues. The people on stage appeared to faint, shout, or fall to the ground, some even convulsing violently.

What in the world is happening here? When did things shift? I hadn't noticed the transition from the pastor's podium to the altar. I looked at my friend and the man beside me. They were both transfixed by the scene unfolding.

And then it happened. The pastor pointed in my direction.

At first, I thought he was pointing at someone behind me, so I turned around. But the people around me were all telling me that he was pointing at *me*. Why? Why on earth would he want *me* to come up to the altar? Was this part of the process of building my relationship with God? Would I have to announce to everyone if I'd met God?

I told my friend I didn't want to go, but she insisted. It was like something out of a scary movie: everyone in the church was suddenly pushing me forward. I was scared. I looked back toward the exit, tempted to make a break for it, but then I saw the pastor, waving for me to come forward.

I slowly stood up, my feet unsure. What was about to

happen? My mind longed to go back to the moment when the music was playing and I was carefree, making up words to songs.

As I walked toward the altar, I was forced to look up at the pastor due to the height of the stage. My nerves were on high alert, sending alarm bells through my body. This was not going to end well.

But even as my stomach twisted, I couldn't help but take inventory of the pastor. Up close, he looked different—better, more authoritative, and confident. He wore a white robe that hid whatever he was wearing underneath, but colorful tassels hung down both sides of his robe, almost like made-to-order doctoral regalia—only with a hood.

His shoes were polished black leather dress shoes, designer-quality, pristine as if they were still new. Draped around his neck with the tassels was a colorful neckerchief that reminded me of something out of a British detective mystery. He wore the whole ensemble with pride, like someone used to being in charge.

Looking him in the eyes, I noticed his brown eyes and overgrown eyebrows. His hair was slightly curly and graying, but it suited him. He had to be in his mid-to-late forties, though his brown skin made his age harder to place.

Then he asked me a question. *"Do you accept the Lord as your Savior?"*

Without hesitation, I replied, *"Yes."* Of course I did— I was just trying to meet Him, to get to know Him better.

Then he asked me the question that caught me off guard: *"Have you been baptized?"*

Whoops. Was that a requirement? I hadn't even thought about it. "No," I replied, and just like that, the room seemed to collectively gasp. I could feel the air shift. The entire congregation seemed to exhale in disappointment. It was as if I'd broken some unspoken rule.

The pastor's face showed clear disappointment. He asked, *"What are you waiting for?"* His voice took on an authoritative tone. *"Why have you put off being baptized?"*

Like a schoolgirl caught in a lie, I stammered, *"I don't know."*

And that's when the tone shifted from uncomfortable to downright dramatic.

The pastor's face tightened with continued disappointment. He raised his palm, and before I could even process what was happening, he struck me on the forehead with a force that shocked me.

"The blood of Jesus commands you! Be baptized in His name!" he shouted.

WHAT THE...?

The hit caused me to frown, at first, because I had no idea why the Pastor was hitting me and shouting at me to be baptized in the name of Jesus. For a moment, I wondered, *Wait, is this Pastor performing an exorcism on me because I haven't been baptized?* Was this some kind of divine retribution? Was Jesus angry with me for not being baptized yet, and now the Pastor was here to deliver some holy punishment on His behalf? The blood of Jesus commanded me to be baptized—whatever that meant.

Before I could even finish those thoughts, the Pastor hit me again, this time harder, landing perfectly on the bridge of my nose.

If you have ever been struck on the bridge of your nose, you know the intense sting that follows. In that instant, tears welled up in my eyes, and he mistook it for some sort of spiritual breakthrough. I was about two seconds away from breaking my fist off in this man's face. My nose was throbbing, and I could feel the anger bubbling inside me, threatening to boil over.

But the Pastor, completely oblivious to my growing fury, was praising God for my *"breakthrough,"* calling out how the Holy Spirit had shaken something loose in me. I stood there, stunned and injured, and if it wasn't for God, Jesus, and the Holy Spirit all working together to stop me, I might have gone to jail that day for physical assault on that Pastor.

I wanted to shout every profane word I could think of, but I swallowed it down. My thoughts were increasingly clear:

I need to leave this church before I get locked up.

As I stepped back to turn and walk away, the Pastor shouted at me, *"Don't run from your demons!"*

Demons? I was tempted to shout back, *the only demon here is you!* But I couldn't even open my mouth to respond, because I was seething with a rage that I knew was dangerous.

My nose was now bleeding, and I could feel my face reddening with anger. A lady sitting near the altar, who had been caught up in the excitement of the moment, noticed the blood and, with surprising gentleness, handed me a tissue. The rest of the church was too consumed with the ecstatic shouts of "Hallelujah!" to notice the blood streaming from my nose, but the lady, bless her, seemed genuinely concerned.

I barely had time to acknowledge her when I heard someone shout from across the room, *"It's in the blood of Jesus!"*

I snapped. *"It's MY blood, because that fool hit me in the nose!"* I shouted, and the words came out of me like a cannon blast.

The people near me froze. I locked eyes with a few individuals in the front row—shocked, wide-eyed, unsure what to make of me. But the rest of the church? They didn't care. They kept shouting. They kept singing. They kept celebrating what they believed to be a spiritual breakthrough—completely oblivious to the fact that my nose was still bleeding, my patience was running thin, and I was on the verge of a full-on meltdown.

Despite the bleeding and the throbbing pain, the Pastor didn't even pause. His voice boomed louder, commanding me to run down the aisle and return to the altar. Three times.

My internal monologue was far less spiritual. *Leave. Leave now. Get out before you do something you'll regret.* But my body was in motion—refusing to do what my mind so desperately wanted: to turn around and make a run for it.

I looked over at my friend, hoping she might give me some sign of reason, but she was completely gone. She was standing there with her eyes closed, her head tilted back like someone in a trance. Her lips were moving, but no sound came out. The church had reached a deafening pitch of excitement, and she appeared to be lost in it all.

I muttered to myself, *God, is this a cult? Will they let me leave without trying to drag me back in?*

By the time I reached the exit doors, I was almost certain I had made it out. I touched my nose, relieved that it wasn't broken—just sore, swollen, and bruised from the impact. But I dared not look back. I was sure that if I did, the entire church would be on my heels, ready to drag me back into their frenzy.

I slipped outside, into the cool air, and made my way to my car. The church doors closed behind me with a finality that felt almost surreal. I wondered, *did anyone even notice I left? Did anyone care that I was bleeding, or were they too caught up in the shouting and the hallelujahs?*

I never looked back. I never returned. And just like that, my friendship with the person who invited me to that church ended, along with any further connection to that place.

It wasn't until years later that I began to understand what happened that day. God had, in fact, met me there. But not because the people in the church ushered Him in. No, He was there because I was there. He used me as a witness to show others—those not lost in the deception—that something was terribly wrong with what was happening under that roof.

God was there to protect me from myself. If it hadn't been for Him, I might have lashed out in anger, but He kept me from committing an act I would have deeply regretted. He showed me that just because someone calls a building a church doesn't mean that it is a place of worship. Just because someone reads from the Bible doesn't mean they have a relationship with God.

The moment I walked out of that church and into my car, I realized something that would shape my faith moving forward: If I was ever going to have a relationship with God, it would need to be a personal one. Not one dictated by man or a building. It would need to be one that I forged with Him, through prayer, through silence, through seeking. But that journey didn't begin right away. It would be many years before I took my first step down that path.

Chapter Three

The Pregnancy

Back in the car, Malachi reached for the radio, and before he could even turn it on, I blurted out, as if he hadn't been sitting in the doctor's office with me just minutes earlier, *"We're having a baby."* He didn't say anything. The silence between us was thick, but it wasn't the kind of silence that invited conversation—it was the kind of silence that screamed, *don't push me right now.*

We both sat there, staring ahead at the stoplight, still not speaking. Then, as if we'd had some unspoken agreement, we both pulled out our phones. It seemed like we were in some kind of unspoken race to inform our mothers about the news, neither of us sure how to start the conversation.

When my mom picked up the phone in California, I couldn't help myself. I had to throw Malachi under the bus. It was almost like I needed to shift the blame. "Mom," I said, "I'm pregnant!" It sounded a little too dramatic, but that was how I felt in the moment.

At the same time, I could hear Malachi telling his mother in Georgia, "Mom, Frankie is pregnant!" He said it like it was all my fault, too—making himself an innocent bystander in this entire mess.

The phone calls that followed were a blur. Both of our mothers were shocked, happy, and scared—all at once. It was like they could hear the mix of fear, excitement, and sheer panic in our voices. We were both still coming to terms with the news, even as we told them, but I couldn't help but notice how different the tone of our conversations was. My mom seemed more supportive, like she'd been expecting this. But Malachi's mom? She seemed like she was still processing.

When the calls finally ended, Malachi pulled into a gas station, killed the engine, and turned to me with the kind of serious look that a cop might give a suspect. He stared me down for a beat before asking, "Are you scared?"

I almost laughed at the question. *Are you serious? Of course, I'm scared. What kind of question is that?* My internal dialogue screamed sarcasm at him: *OF COURSE NOT, I'VE DONE THIS PLENTY OF TIMES. THIS IS NOTHING.*

But I didn't say any of that. I just nodded. "Yes."

Malachi sighed deeply and then asked, "Are you happy?"

It was strange—despite the shock, despite the fear, I could feel something else creeping in. It was joy, subtle but undeniable. I smiled. "Yes. I'm happy," I said, surprised by the sincerity in my own voice.

He looked at me and smiled back, nodding his head, "I'm happy too."

But even then, it wasn't all happiness. It was a tangled mess of emotions—joy, fear, anxiety, excitement, and even dread. I wasn't sure how to process it all. Was this really happening?

Malachi stepped out of the car to pay for gas and grab some snacks. "Want anything specific?" he asked.

I shrugged, "Anything you bring will do." I wasn't really hungry, but I could tell I was stalling for time. I didn't want to be alone in my thoughts right now.

I watched him walk into the gas station, feeling like the world outside the car had somehow changed. There was something almost surreal about the moment. I was looking at everything as if it were for the first time—the colors of the trees, the noise of the cars, the people walking by. The crisp fall air outside the car made me feel like I was somewhere far removed from the concrete of downtown Atlanta. For a few seconds in my mind, I wasn't in a car in a gas station parking lot. I was in some peaceful mountain retreat. It was enough to momentarily calm my swirling thoughts.

When Malachi returned, he was holding a bag bulging with snacks, like it was Christmas morning. I couldn't help but smile. He clearly thought he'd hit the jackpot with whatever goodies he'd grabbed. I let my mind wander as I thought about the snacks in the bag. I was kind of looking forward to seeing what he picked.

He slid into the driver's seat, eager to share. "You're going to love this!" he said, practically beaming.

I grabbed the bag and started rifling through it. There were two of everything I could imagine. A bottle of water, some chips, a candy bar, and then—yes, the pretzels. My snack of choice. I dug in, feeling a little more grounded as the salt and crunch settled my nerves.

On the way home, I couldn't help but think about what had just happened—how my life had shifted in an instant. I wasn't just Frankie anymore. I wasn't just a woman figuring it all out. I was pregnant. I was going to be a mother.

When I got home and started getting ready for the evening, I passed by the bathroom mirror. And there it was. A little bump. Not just gas, not just bloating, but my baby. My internal monologue went into overdrive, my mind flooded with a combination of pride, fear, and utter disbelief.

I'm going to be a mother. The weight of it hit me all at once, and suddenly, the tears were coming—unexpected, uncontrolled.

Malachi, hearing me cry from the other room, rushed in, probably thinking something was wrong. He leaned in the doorway, looking worried. "Are you okay?" he asked.

I quickly wiped my tears. "I'm fine. I'm just scared." I wasn't crying because I wasn't happy; I was crying because this was real. *This was really happening.*

He walked over, put his arms around me, and kissed the top of my head. "Me too. But we're going to be okay. I love you. I love our baby. I can't wait to meet Malachi or Frankie Junior!"

His goofy grin spread across his face, and for a moment, I was caught off guard. But I couldn't help it—I laughed. We both laughed, and it made everything feel a little lighter. It wasn't going to be easy, but we were in this together. And for the first time, I felt a glimmer of hope that maybe, just maybe, we could make it work.

In the months that followed, Malachi kept his word— he attended every doctor's appointment his schedule allowed. But ironically, while we were both invested in the baby, our marriage wasn't weathering the storm as well. We were living separate lives in many ways. My pregnancy became the center of our lives, but outside of that, it felt like we were two people coexisting rather than partners.

The doctor had told me the pregnancy would last around nine months, but it felt like it had been years already. I mean, had it really only been a few months? Some days, I felt like I'd been pregnant for at least twenty-four months, with no end in sight.

I'd try to remind myself to stop complaining. I had a relatively easy pregnancy—no morning sickness lasting more than a couple of days, some odd cravings (like sushi with ketchup and mustard—don't ask), a little swelling here and there—nothing serious. Yet, every time I looked down at my ankles, it felt like I was wearing 1980s leg warmers made of skin. The swelling made me laugh a little, but then my inner monologue reminded me to count my blessings. My pregnancy could have been much worse.

I had a sporadic bout of vertigo during my pregnancy that would hit me every time I ascended or descended the stairs in our home. It wasn't just disorienting; it was downright terrifying. More than once, I nearly fell up the stairs. Yes, up! It sounds ridiculous, but it happened. Going down was bad enough, but when I'd imagine an extra step and move to take it—only to realize there wasn't one—it felt like the universe was playing a cruel trick on me.

The worst part? I was alone when it happened. Every single time. I couldn't help but imagine what would happen if I *did* fall. Would I break something? Would I hurt the baby? Thankfully, I never did fall—down or up—but the episodes left me shaken each time.

Aside from the vertigo, there were the typical pregnancy complaints—minor backaches, swollen ankles, and cravings. But the one medical issue that took me by surprise? The agony of impacted bowels. If you're unfamiliar with the term, count yourself lucky, because I'm not going to relive that trauma for you. Let's just say that it was the kind of discomfort that required a doctor's intervention, and once it was taken care of, I could return to the bliss of pregnancy...minus the bowel issues. I have to admit, though, that despite the discomforts, I would gladly choose this pregnancy all over again (except for that one detail).

But let's talk about those swollen ankles for a second. As much as they were a natural part of pregnancy, I also played a role in their swelling. See, I refused to quit my job at the university, and I insisted on parking what felt like 27,000 miles from my office. Okay, maybe not that far, but it was definitely about three blocks away. Now, three blocks doesn't sound like much to most people, but trust me, to a pregnant woman— especially one in Georgia's summer heat and humidity—it feels like a marathon.

Have you ever spent a summer in the South? If you have, you know exactly what I'm talking about. If not, imagine this: You're in a storage unit in the middle of the desert. The doors are sealed, but there's a constant stream of water being poured on it, evaporating the second it hits the ground. That's summer in Georgia.

One morning, as I sat in my car, looking down at my belly—now almost touching the steering wheel—I realized I was probably pushing the limit on when I should still be driving myself. The doctor had warned me about when it would be unsafe for me to continue, but that day, I wasn't ready to give up my independence just yet.

As I sat there, pondering whether to turn the car back on and head home, my thoughts quickly shifted to the cafeteria. *It's Mexican food day!* I had been looking forward to it all week, and there was no way I was going to miss out on that feast. But as the idea of walking three blocks in the sweltering heat hit me, I felt a wave of exhaustion wash over me. I wanted to cry. *Why is it so humid today? How did I get here?* And yet, despite the self-pity, I remembered that glorious Mexican food was waiting for me.

So, with a sigh, I pushed the door open and started my trek. By the time I reached the second block, the baby had decided to press its entire weight against my bladder, and suddenly, I found myself humming the theme to *Rocky* just to keep my spirits up. I felt like I needed some sort of soundtrack to my struggle. When I finally made it to the nearest building, I dashed in, practically screaming, "Where's the bathroom?!"

The shocked looks on the faces of the people inside didn't faze me. I just needed to go. As I was directed to the bathroom, I couldn't resist shouting back over my shoulder, "Thank you! It's Mexican food day in the cafeteria!" They just stared at me blankly, probably wondering if they should call for help.

When I made it to the office, my coworkers were already waiting for me. "Ms. Prego is never late," I overheard one of them say as I rounded the corner. I felt the need to announce my arrival—because, you know, no one could see that I'd made it—along with an explanation of my bathroom pitstop and, of course, the fact that it was *Mexican food day.*

One of my coworkers, who had clearly become attuned to my pregnancy cravings, showed me my calendar—complete with a reminder for Mexican food day, as if I'd ever forget. It was like a sacred ritual at this point. And sure enough, a few of us ventured to the cafeteria, where I fueled up for the day with round two of breakfast. Breakfast part one had been at home, but this was a whole different level. We're talking tacos, burritos, refried beans, cheese, onions—the whole spread. By the time I had walked those three blocks in the oppressive Georgia humidity, I had burned through enough calories to make Mexican food *necessary* for survival.

But beyond the food, it was the perks of pregnancy that I started to notice. As a regular in the cafeteria, the staff knew me by name, knew when I was due, and by now, they were in tune with my schedule. The staff made sure to have a little something extra for me every time I walked in—sometimes fruit, sometimes pastries—always accompanied by water. I shared whatever treats I got with my coworkers since they didn't have the luxury of being spoiled by the cafeteria staff. It was one of the few perks of being *Ms. Prego.*

Back at the office, I sat at my desk, enjoying breakfast

part two while everyone else was running around—answering phones, filing papers, dealing with students. I felt a little guilty, but at the same time, I embraced the laziness. I mean, they were practically *worshiping* me at this point. One coworker brought over a chair and a pillow so I could prop up my swollen feet while another came by with a cold bottle of water, urging me to stay hydrated. It was like being pampered in the middle of the workday. If I could stay pregnant forever—especially with reserved parking and a cafeteria that catered to my every craving—I would have been all for it.

Of course, the perks didn't stop there. As I waddled my way back from the ladies' room, one of my coworkers met me in what we affectionately called the *cruise ship hallway*—because it was wide enough for several people to walk comfortably without bumping into each other. The carpet had this funky, wavy pattern, and the artwork on the walls, while not exactly Picasso, had a certain charm to it.

My coworker gave me a curious look as I approached, clearly wondering how I was doing. I paused for a second, considering his question. But instead of answering, I switched gears completely. "Mexican food day's coming up, you know," I said, my hormones switching tracks without hesitation.

He caught on and, sensing my hormonal shift, offered an alternative suggestion: "We've still got thirty minutes before lunch. If you want, we can grab a snack while we wait."

And so, the cycle of pregnancy pampering continued.

That day marked the last time I'd ever enjoy Mexican food day in the cafeteria. For the record, the food was absolutely delicious. The tacos were seasoned to perfection, the burritos were stuffed just right, and don't even get me started on the refried beans and cheese. It was the type of meal that made you feel like life was a little better, a little easier, and just *right*—until it wasn't.

Because less than twenty minutes after finishing my feast, I started to feel it. The swelling hit me hard, like an unexpected wave. My ankles, which had already been under stress from the Georgia heat and my own poor parking choices, began to swell up in a way that made me think of those high-quality 1980s legwarmers. The ones that were made from that thick, knitted fabric that your mom used to buy for you when you were a kid, only these ones were *tight*. Tight to the point where they almost felt like they were cutting off circulation.

I could feel my hands starting to tingle, too—like they'd been left out in the snow for too long and then someone decided to warm them up a little too quickly by putting on a pair of fuzzy gloves. You know that odd, prickly sensation? Yeah, that was happening to my hands. And then there were my wrists—so swollen that I didn't even realize it until my coworker asked me about it. I had been washing my hands in the ladies' room when I noticed that my wrists had started to puff up, but I didn't give it much thought. Who does? I had a million other things on my mind—like whether or not I'd made it back to my office before the lunch rush.

But when he asked how I was feeling, it hit me. I looked at my hands and wrists again and realized they weren't just puffy—they were *inflated*. At that moment, I had the urge to report to my coworkers the full extent of my swollen condition—*"Look! I have sausage fingers!"*—but I decided against it. There's a certain amount of pride you try to hold onto when you're in the office, even when you're several months pregnant. So, instead of going into a full, hormonal breakdown about how my body was slowly turning into a balloon, I quietly returned to my desk, kicked my feet up, and tried to get some work done.

It was hard to concentrate. Every time I tried to type on the computer, I had to look down at my now *full-grown pumpkin-sized hands* and think, *how am I even going to press these keys?* It was as if my fingers were swollen sausages, too big to even curl around the keyboard properly. But I soldiered on. I tried to enter data, despite the tingling sensation in my hands and the throbbing in my feet. I was determined to finish the day without anyone noticing how uncomfortable I was. But I couldn't focus. All I could think about was the *walk* I'd have to make back to my car—because, of course, I had parked three blocks away from the office, as usual.

I sat in my chair, trying to finish a few more tasks before the day ended, but the thought of walking back to my car hung over me like an insurmountable mountain. Three blocks in the heat. Three blocks with swollen ankles and hands. Three blocks, while my bladder screamed for relief. The mere idea of it felt like torture.

For the rest of the afternoon, I shifted in my chair every few minutes, trying to relieve the pressure building in my lower body. My coworkers worked around me, chatting about their day, asking how I was doing, but I just smiled through it. I didn't want to admit how badly I was struggling. I didn't want to admit that, yes, I was pregnant—wonderful and terrifying—but right now, it felt like too much. Too much swelling. Too much pressure. Too much of everything.

When it was finally time to go, I stood gingerly, testing my swollen ankles with each step. My legs felt heavy, and my feet felt like they were encased in concrete. I silently cursed the universe for the three-block walk, then reminded myself I was being ridiculous. I was pregnant, not dying. I could do this. I had no choice but to do this.

Taking a deep breath, I started the walk back to my car. My steps slowed, and every movement felt exaggerated. The sidewalks seemed to stretch farther than I remembered, the air heavier, the sun hotter. My body wasn't cooperating, but I pushed through.

As I approached my car, I noticed a small, relieved sigh escape my lips. The distance from the office to the parking lot felt like a lifetime, but I had made it. I reached my car, opened the door, and collapsed into the seat with a sense of victory. As I sat there, trying to catch my breath and let the reality of my body settle, I realized one thing for sure: I had no idea how I was going to make it through the next several months.

But I wasn't going to give up. I couldn't. I was carrying a life inside me, and no amount of swollen ankles, tingly hands, or Mexican-food-induced discomfort could change that.

Still, I swore to myself that the next time Mexican food day came around, I'd either stay home or just *maybe* opt for a salad. My body—and my swollen ankles—deserved better.

But in that moment, all I wanted was to get home, prop my feet up, and give my body the rest it desperately needed before tomorrow's challenges began again.

Chapter Four

Is It Time Yet

As the weeks passed, I found myself caught up in a whirlwind of preparations for the arrival of my little one. The baby shower circuit was in full swing, and I was lucky enough to have two celebrations—one with my work family and the other with my actual family. Both were filled with love, laughter, and well-meaning advice, though each had its own unique flavor. But the work baby shower? That's where I have to start, because honestly, it felt like an extension of the emotional highs and lows I'd been experiencing throughout my pregnancy.

My work family shower was catered by the cafeteria staff, and yes, you guessed it—Mexican food made its grand return. By then, I had long since grown tired of it. My taste buds had rebelled against the spicy nachos and enchiladas. I was over it. I craved comfort food—Southern comfort food. The kind that could be fried, smothered, or baked. I dreamed of smothered pork chops, macaroni and cheese, collard greens, hot buttery biscuits, and yams. That was the food that spoke to my soul, especially with the sweltering Georgia heat weighing down on me like an invisible force.

But the Mexican food? I couldn't bring myself to share

that with anyone. After all, the shower was for the baby, and I didn't want to be the one to kill the vibe with a "Oh, I'm so over this now!" So, I pushed aside my craving for Southern goodness, put on my best "this is great!" face, and dug in— even though my heart wasn't in it. *Mexican food, once a beloved treat, now felt like a chore.*

The baby shower itself was limited to two hours. A small window, really, but enough to squeeze in a game and some socializing. The game was something like "Guess the Baby Item" or "Guess How Big the Baby Bump Is" — standard fare for any office baby shower. The food was available for the entire workday, but we didn't have time for much more than that one game. I could tell that the clock was ticking down quickly on this limited time window, but what really stretched it out was the prayer.

Now, I am all for taking a moment of silence and gratitude, but the person who was asked to pray over the food? Well, he had the longest prayer I'd ever experienced. By the time he finished, I was fairly certain we had used up about an hour and a half of our allotted two hours. My thoughts wandered, as they often do when you're physically drained and emotionally spent. I could barely focus on his words, and instead, my mind drifted back to another, more peculiar experience I had during my spiritual journey.

Years before, I had been invited by a friend to attend

her church. She promised that I would love it, that it would be "such a great experience," and I was, of course, all in. At that time, I was genuinely seeking a deeper understanding of God—who He was, and who I was in relation to Him. But I should have known better when her only pitch was, "You'll love it." *Love it?* What was that supposed to mean?

I arrived at the church, and immediately, I was struck by its sheer grandeur. The building was breathtaking. It looked like something straight out of Italy, a Gothic masterpiece nestled in the middle of a metropolitan city. I found myself mesmerized by its beauty. The intricately carved pews, the tall, wax-covered candlesticks standing at attention in various corners of the sanctuary, and the majestic stained-glass windows that bathed the room in a spectrum of vibrant colors. It was as if every inch of the space had been carefully designed to invoke awe.

As I made my way deeper into the church, I tried to take in every detail. It was so ornate that it almost didn't seem real. When I finally sat down with my friend, I couldn't help but mention how magnificent the building was. She was naturally proud and assured me that the congregation was equally welcoming and warm, encouraging me to stick around after the service to chat with anyone who wanted to talk. My inner monologue, however, questioned whether the whole congregation was dying to chat with me or if it was just a few select people.

Then the service began, and the grandeur of the building quickly faded into the backdrop as the ritual of kneeling and standing took center stage. I tried to keep up with the rest of the congregation, but my knees were definitely not on board with the program. I managed to kneel once before I gave up, staying seated while everyone else knelt and chanted. The rhythm was soothing in a way, but also a little bewildering. I was just trying to figure out the next step in the sequence, like a bad dancer at a wedding reception.

And then, it happened.

The priest made a statement that made me sit up straighter in my seat, looking around to see if anyone else was reacting. Surely, I couldn't have been the only one who heard him? He said, "The only way to get to heaven is to come to church several times a week, confess your sins to me—not to God—and give money to the church."

Wait, what?

I froze, the words echoing in my mind. I wasn't a theologian, but even in my limited understanding of faith at that point in my life, I knew that something wasn't right. The idea that I had to go through a human intermediary to confess my sins, that I had to give money to this church, and that simply attending services regularly would somehow guarantee me access to heaven—it didn't sit well with me.

I reached into my purse and pulled out my light blue pocket-sized Bible. I began flipping through it, searching for verses that might clarify the matter. The church, too, had provided a Bible in the pew in front of me, so I cross-referenced what I found in my small Bible with what was written in the church-provided version. I wasn't out to start a theological debate right then and there, but something told me that I had to find the truth for myself.

I won't drag you through every scripture I found, but suffice it to say, I uncovered several truths that left me feeling both liberated and a bit unsettled. The Priest's words did not line up with what the Bible actually said. I discovered that salvation, in its purest form, doesn't hinge on the number of church services you attend or the amount of money you give to the church. It's about a personal relationship with God, one that doesn't require a middleman. Confession? According to scripture, I can confess directly to God. And as for giving? While generosity is encouraged, it is not a requirement to earn God's favor.

I walked away from that church service that day with a profound sense of peace. The truth, as they say, will set you free, and that was exactly what happened. The priest's teachings didn't resonate with me, but my own search for the truth led me to a deeper understanding of faith—one that was grounded not in rituals, but in a personal connection with God.

As I returned to the present moment at my baby shower, with its Mexican food and overly long prayer, I couldn't help but smile inwardly. The journey I had taken, both physically and spiritually, had given me a perspective that not everyone would share—but it was mine. And it was enough.

Before I move on to the family baby shower, I need to pause for a moment on the reflections I had as I went through my personal spiritual journey. Those moments of self-doubt, soul-searching, and those quiet realizations that came from studying Scripture on my own — all of it formed the foundation for a much deeper understanding of what truly mattered in life. I had read verses like John 3:16, Romans 10:9-10, and Ephesians 2:8-9, all of which pointed to one undeniable truth: salvation, and ultimately, entry into heaven, comes through belief in Jesus Christ and not through human rituals, physical attendance at church services, or financial offerings.

To be fair, I'm no biblical scholar, and I'm not writing a theology book here. But the process of searching for answers on my own, digging into the Bible and questioning what I had been taught, proved invaluable. My heart knew that the gospel was simple: It's by grace, through faith, and through Jesus alone. No priest, no amount of money, and no set of actions could earn me salvation. And as I discovered, confession wasn't about a middleman — it was between me and God.

I was determined that if nothing else, I would continue learning and building a relationship with God. And when I left that church that day, I left with more clarity and peace than I had ever experienced.

And now, back to the baby shower…

By the time I arrived at my family's baby shower, I was ready for some relief — not just from the swollen ankles, but from the endless advice and questions I had been bombarded with during the work shower. That was when I realized just how much I'd been craving a break, and how precious a bit of quiet time could be. But my sister-in-law and mother-in-law were ready to throw down in the kitchen and set everything up beautifully for the occasion. I was grateful they were handling the details; I could barely handle my feet at this point.

The swollen ankles were ridiculous. I had already made multiple trips to the car, each one more painful than the last. By the time I made it into the house, I felt like I had lead in my legs. My ankles were so tight they felt like a pair of constricting socks, with an added layer of weight as if I was wearing ankle weights. *Relief* was all I wanted at that point, but it wasn't coming soon enough.

But, as I walked into the house, I was greeted with warmth and love from my in-laws, many of whom I had grown close to over the years. They made me feel like part of their family, despite being so far from my own. It was a comfort, especially since I was about to face yet another round of questions from people I didn't know very well.

A woman I didn't recognize suddenly approached me, rattling off a string of personal questions. When was I due? Was this my first baby? Did I have any *major pregnancy issues?* Now, I'm not sure what "major pregnancy issues" were in her mind, but the way she said it made me feel like I should get a physical exam on the spot. I was so thrown off that I didn't even answer her in full. I simply answered her questions in the order she asked them. I informed her that I had no "major pregnancy issues" (because honestly, what did she mean by that?), and I left it at that.

There was a moment when I thought about revealing some of my "issues" — like the swelling in my ankles (which I blamed on bad shoes or the cafeteria's Mexican food), or how my bowels had decided to stage a protest for several days. But, I quickly shut it down. This wasn't the time or place to start a medical conversation and again, who is this lady?

Then, the conversation took another turn — a question about my weight gain. How much weight had I gained?

With a smile, I proudly announced, "I've actually lost fifteen pounds!" I could see the shock on her face. Most people gain weight during pregnancy, but I hadn't, and it was something I had been reassured by my doctor was perfectly fine. My pregnancy wasn't typical in some ways, but I knew the baby and I were both healthy. But the woman's reaction — wide-eyed and worried — was something I wasn't quite ready for.

She proceeded to scold me with a tone that was very condescending, "Young lady, you just make sure you take care of yourself! That baby is depending on you!" She walked away, no doubt thinking I was some sort of a neglectful mother-to-be. Initially I was going to school her about my health and pregnancy; however, I allowed her to walk away with her sense of achievement in diagnosing my pregnancy and what I needed to do with my body.

Pregnancy is full of uninformed assumptions and unsolicited advice, and I had learned quickly that the best response is often silence.

By this time, the baby shower games had fully kicked off, and it seemed like every other person had a question or piece of advice. It became overwhelming at times, but I didn't let it bother me. After all, it was a celebration of new life, of love and support — and I was grateful for the kind-hearted people surrounding me.

At one point, I casually mentioned to the group that the pregnancy had helped me focus more on eating healthier. *Well, aside from the occasional splurge on Mexican food at work,* I added, remembering how often I'd paid the price for my indulgence. But there was something about this baby that felt like a complete lifestyle change. I was even convinced that I was going to have an all-natural birth — no drugs, no interventions — just like women in the old days. I had convinced myself that the water birth trend was the way to go, and I was certain I could do it.

Little did I know, though...

As the day went on, the men at the shower — Malachi included — were getting their fill of food and football. There was an oversized flat-screen TV downstairs where the fellas had already gathered. My husband was clearly more interested in watching the game than playing baby shower games, but I could hardly blame him. It was the same way he'd shown up for every family event: A little bit of presence, a lot of food, and then a quick escape to the nearest TV.

I found myself watching him, along with the other men, head downstairs in their typical fashion — laughing, carrying plates, and talking among themselves. In that moment, I realized this might be what parenting looked like in the future. There would be moments when I would be surrounded by family and friends, handling the details and the emotional weight of parenthood while Malachi and the guys would be content with the simpler pleasures of life: food, football, and a little bit of escape.

I smiled, though, because at the end of the day, that's

what life is about — finding balance. The balance between sacrifice and enjoyment, between nurturing and letting go. I knew this would be my reality as a mother. And as I waddled back to my seat, ankles still swollen, I felt a sense of peace. I was surrounded by love, support, and a deep sense of gratitude for the family I had — both blood and chosen.

And in that moment, the true meaning of family became clearer than ever.

Chapter Five

The Waiting Game

The excitement of discovering that our little "peanut" was a boy quickly transformed into a mix of overwhelming joy and deep reflection. Within just a few weeks, I had gone from feeling lighthearted and hopeful about the future to confronting the harsh realities of the world around me. The tragic events of September 11, 2001, shook me to my core. Sitting there, curled up on the stairs, my heart ached for those who had lost their lives, for their families, and for a world that now seemed much more dangerous and uncertain.

My heart was torn in two directions: on one hand, I felt immense love for the little life growing inside of me, but on the other, I wondered what kind of world he was being born into. Would he be safe? Would I be able to protect him from the horrors of the world? As I cried and apologized to my unborn son, promising to do my best to shield him from the evils I was witnessing, I could almost feel him respond. His little kicks — the ones that had already become so familiar to me — felt like his way of reassuring me that no matter how dark the world seemed, he was a bright light of hope in our lives.

In that moment of emotional turmoil, the baby kicked

again. This time, the force of his movement was enough to make my nightshirt flare out as he pressed against my bladder. The physical reminder of his presence was like a gentle nudge, signaling that despite the sadness I was feeling, there was still a precious life growing inside of me. I didn't know how to explain it, but it felt like a sign that we would get through this — that I would be able to hold onto hope, for his sake.

In the midst of it all, I found myself reminiscing about lighter times. I remembered the week before when my brother, Danin, and I had been watching football, joking about the name for the baby. What seemed to be out of nowhere, the name Donovan had appeared on the screen during the game, and in a moment of whimsy, I blurted the name out to my brother. He thought it was "cool," and just like that, it was settled. I decided to run it by Malachi, and when I did, he immediately agreed, but suggested we spell it differently. Our son would be named Donovin Malachi Stokes — a name that felt strong, unique, and perfect.

Out of excitement, we laughed about it, and in my mind, I pictured Donovin growing up with that name — playing sports, making friends, facing challenges, living his life. I touched my stomach and whispered his name, as if to tell him that it was final. In response, he gave me a little wiggle, as if acknowledging that he approved of his name. I chuckled at the thought. How funny that I was already learning so much about this little person — his personality, his quirks — even before he was born.

The days leading up to his birth weren't as calm as I had imagined, especially since the pregnancy journey up to this point had been calm. On the morning of October 27, 2001, Malachi was up early, and I had spent the night tossing and turning. I didn't focus much on Malachi's early morning activities. I was too preoccupied with the strange and uncomfortable sensations I was feeling in my body. My stomach was tight, and I felt a heavy, strange pressure building.

And then it happened: a contraction. It was faint at first, barely noticeable. But as it came and went, I remembered what they had taught us in birthing class — that early contractions would feel like strong menstrual cramps. I would have gladly traded the "discomfort" for that experience in a heartbeat, because this pain was far from a mere cramp. It radiated through my abdomen like a thunderclap, and as it intensified, it was clear to me that this wasn't just a drill. This was it.

Malachi, sweet and calm as ever, brought me breakfast in bed. But when he entered the room, he was walking into a storm, and I was its eye. The peaceful morning, we had planned quickly descended into chaos as the contractions hit harder, faster, and more frequently. I was no longer a woman in labor; I was a woman in agony.

"CALL THE HOSPITAL!" I screamed at Malachi, my voice shaking with urgency. His response was bewildered, asking me if I was sure. *Was I in labor?* I gave him a look that could have frozen him in his tracks — a look that screamed, "Of course I'm in labor, why else would I be screaming like this?" But even with the pain radiating through my body, I knew I needed to stay calm for the sake of our baby, for the sake of Malachi.

He called the hospital. And I'll never forget the nurse's voice on the other end of the line. She asked me the usual questions: Was this my first baby? Had my water broken? How far apart were the contractions? But before I could answer, another wave of pain hit me, and I'm pretty sure I screamed into the phone. "I'M IN LABOR!" I don't even know how the nurse managed to stay calm, but she did. Her voice was the only steady thing in the madness.

After that phone call, there was no turning back. We were going to the hospital, no questions asked.

But it wasn't the calm, collected moment I had expected. We had rushed to the hospital weeks before, only to be sent home because it wasn't yet time. This time, however, it was clear: the baby was coming.

I was terrified. Terrified of the pain. Terrified of what was to come. And yet, at the same time, there was excitement. I was about to meet my son, the little boy I had already fallen in love with. But first, I had to survive the labor. And if the contractions were any indication, this was going to be one long, painful journey.

As Malachi and I made our way to Northside Hospital, I felt a mix of emotions. I wasn't ready for this, and yet, I was. I had spent nine months preparing for this moment — or so I thought. But nothing could prepare me for the intensity of labor, or for the overwhelming love I would feel when I finally held my son in my arms.

Donovin Malachi Stokes was on his way — and nothing, not even the fear or the pain, could stop that now.

As I lay there, feeling like I was about to burst with each passing contraction, the surrealness of it all hit me. The calmness of the nurse on the other end of the phone felt almost comical, a stark contrast to the whirlwind of emotions and pain I was enduring. When she confirmed that I was indeed about to have my baby, it was as if a switch flipped in my brain — the reality of it all came crashing down. I was going to give birth, and there was no turning back.

The "this is not a drill" feeling hit me hard, and I burst into tears. It was a mixture of fear, excitement, and the overwhelming weight of knowing that life as I knew it was about to change forever. There was no turning back. I was about to become a mother.

I don't think I even realized how slow Malachi was

driving until we hit a bump in the road and another contraction ame. Malachi, who had driven countless times before, suddenly seemed to forget what speed was. We crawled along, barely able to get above 25 miles per hour, even as semis zoomed past us, honking their horns. I couldn't decide whether I was more upset about holding up traffic or about every bump and jolt in the road triggering a new wave of contractions.

At one point, the road ahead narrowed into a construction zone, and I was certain I was going to have that baby in the backseat of the car. I thought about jumping out and running the rest of the way to the hospital — at least then, I wouldn't risk having a baby on the side of the highway. Even though the thought made me giggle briefly, I couldn't move, not with contractions starting to feel like someone was twisting my insides.

Finally, after what felt like hours, we arrived at the hospital. The staff whisked me away, moving with purpose that gave me the briefest feeling of hope. It was like stepping into a movie scene, where everything was happening at lightning speed, and I was the star of it all. They sat me in a wheelchair and rushed me through double doors, passing other women in labor, each on their own journey — some crying, some shouting, others looking serene (which, let's be honest, was probably just the medication talking).

When I finally settled into my delivery room, I felt like

I was in a luxurious hotel room, or at least that was how I wanted to think of it in my delirious, pain-filled state. The room was spacious, with a full-sized bed and a sitting area that seemed more fitting for a family gathering than the chaos of childbirth. The bathroom was larger than my own at home, and I briefly wondered if this was what "hospital chic" was supposed to feel like. Still, all I cared about was that I was in a safe place, and the professionals around me were taking good care of me.

As I lay there, trying to calm myself between contractions, a fleeting sadness washed over me. My mom was on her way from California, but I didn't know if she would make it in time. As I thought about her, a wave of emotion hit me again — here I was, about to bring my son into the world, and my mom wasn't here to witness it. It was a sobering thought, but then, just as quickly, a strange sense of relief swept over me. I was still going through this process, still here, and still strong. And then, just to make everything feel more like *me*, **COPS** came on TV.

I watched the officers chase down criminals, all while silently hoping my own chase would soon end — this labor was definitely starting to feel like a criminal pursuit. Between contractions, I even allowed myself the briefest moments of humor. For some reason, watching the police handle chaotic situations was helping me breathe through the madness in my own life.

Soon, my mother-in-law Leslie and my sister-in-law Kina arrived, and suddenly, I was surrounded by my family — my support system — all ready to witness this little one's grand entrance. At first, I felt slightly overwhelmed by their presence. It was as if I was the center of a storm, with my in-laws watching on in hushed anticipation. I noticed how calm and composed my mother-in-law was — almost too composed. Leslie was a woman who took charge of everything, and seeing her so quiet, so still, was unsettling at first. But then I understood. She was giving me the space to experience the moment on my own terms, to have this moment of motherhood without interference. She wasn't being weak — she was being strong in a way I hadn't expected.

Kina, on the other hand, was right there by my side. She was the first to jump in, holding my hand, bringing me ice chips, and even helping me with one of my legs when the time came to push. She was fierce and loving, and I was so grateful for her strength. She was my anchor in that room, keeping me grounded when I felt like I might float away from the pain and fear.

Malachi, sweet Malachi, was also by my side. I could tell he was doing his best to remain calm and collected, but the truth was, he was *freaking out*. I could see it in his eyes. He helped me into the shower, where the warm water provided a brief, comforting reprieve from the increasingly painful contractions. As the water flowed over me, I tried to focus on the sensation of calm, tried to hold onto the small semblance of peace before the storm of pushing and labor came crashing down. But the pain continued to intensify, the contractions feeling more like someone was reaching into my body and twisting my organs.

And then it hit me — *this is real.* I was truly about to give birth. And yet, for a moment, my mind drifted away from the pain and fear. I could hear the distant cries of another woman, someone down the hall or maybe even in another wing. Her screams echoed through the building, and for a moment, I forgot about my own suffering. Her pain was so raw, so unfiltered, that it almost became a distraction. I felt sorry for her, but more than that, I felt connected to her. She, too, was going through this impossible thing. This thing called motherhood.

As her cries reverberated through the hallways, I realized that I wasn't alone. Even if I felt like I was the only one in that room, there were others going through the same experience, in their own rooms, in their own ways. We were all, in some way, connected by the pain and the joy that comes with bringing life into the world. And as I lay there, bracing for the next wave of contractions, I knew one thing for sure: I wasn't just giving birth to Donovin. I was becoming a mother, just like every other woman before me who had walked this painful, beautiful, and transformative path.

Chapter Six

Donovin Has Arrived

The pain, confusion, and uncertainty all seemed to fade into the background the moment the doctor entered the room again. He checked my progress, his brow furrowed in what I could only assume was professional concern, then asked me the question that would change everything: "Do you want an epidural?"

At that exact moment, another contraction surged through me like a freight train, and I had to summon every ounce of willpower not to scream at him. "Yes!" I yelled, almost desperately, as the contraction hit. There was no time for further conversation; the pain had completely commandeered the room. I no longer cared what anyone else said or did — I was locked into the rhythm of the contraction, the only thing that mattered in that moment.

Then, just as quickly as the pain had flared, Doctor Make Me Feel Good walked in, and everything shifted again. In the midst of the agony, I found myself noticing him in a way I probably shouldn't have. I mean, come on — it was hard to ignore a doctor who could easily double as a model. His chiseled jaw, perfectly styled brown hair, dazzling smile, and skin that looked like it belonged in an advertisement all blurred together in my mind. But this wasn't just any doctor — this was the doctor who could give me the one thing I needed more than anything: relief.

I'm not sure what he said, or if I even understood him, but I remember nodding and agreeing to everything. I was so focused on the fact that he was about to ease my pain that I could barely process his words. When he asked again if I wanted the epidural, I managed to confirm through gritted teeth that I did, and that I would really appreciate it before the next contraction. He smiled that dreamy smile of his, and I could almost hear the angels singing.

And then... the epidural. Let's take a moment to talk about that.

At first, it felt like a sharp pain shooting through my back, and my focus immediately shifted from my brief fascination with Doctor Make Me Feel Good to the extreme discomfort of a needle being shoved into my spine. I don't know if the needle was huge or if my pain tolerance just completely crumbled, but it hurt — a lot. The world seemed to spin a little as I tried to focus on not moving, as instructed, while the needle did its thing, but as soon as it was done, relief flooded my body. The epidural wasn't a miracle, but it was close. I couldn't feel anything from the waist down anymore, and the harsh waves of contractions were replaced with a warm, almost soothing sensation that spread through my lower half.

As I lay there, disconnected from my own body, I looked at the monitors and saw the contractions still coming, still increasing in intensity. But all I could feel was warmth and a weird sense of calm. I began to question why any woman would not choose the epidural. The pain of childbirth seemed ridiculous in comparison to the comfort of a drug that allowed me to focus on anything other than my own body betraying me.

That is, until I felt my legs begin to shake uncontrollably. It was the strangest, most disconcerting sensation — like my legs had taken on a life of their own. The shaking was so intense that my family rushed to my side, holding my hands and reassuring me that this was just another side effect of the epidural. They kept telling me it was normal, but all I wanted was for it to stop.

And then, as if the shaking wasn't enough, I suddenly felt freezing cold. I shivered uncontrollably as my body was covered with not one, not two, but four blankets. I was simultaneously numb, shaking, and freezing, and it was a bizarre combination of sensations that made me feel like I was in some weird dream.

But as the shaking finally subsided and my body settled, the urge to do something became overwhelming. Watching the contractions on the monitor was fascinating for about five minutes, but soon I was growing bored, restless. I wanted to push. I wanted to meet my son.

And then, like a divine intervention, the doctor walked back into the room, looked at the monitors, looked at me, and declared, "It's time to push."

I could barely contain my excitement. Maybe it was the epidural, or maybe it was just sheer exhaustion, but I smiled at him with what could only be described as a psychotic enthusiasm, saying, "Oooookkkk!" I'm sure it wasn't the most graceful or eloquent response, but I didn't care. I was ready. Donovin was coming, and nothing was going to stop him.

By now, I had completely given up on waiting for my mom to arrive. I had wanted her there so badly, but I realized that I couldn't wait any longer, Donovin Malachi Stokes wasn't going to allow it. The childbirth train had left the station, and I wasn't going to miss it. The excitement was electric. This was it. My son was about to be born.

The room had become a whirlwind of activity. Nurses and doctors moved around me with practiced efficiency, and I could hear the buzz of conversation and the sounds of medical equipment, but it all felt distant, as if I were watching it from underwater. The moment had come, and everything was in motion.

Then, the pressure. A pressure so intense, it felt like I was about to explode. The doctor instructed me to push, and without a second thought, I did. The world narrowed to that one singular effort, pushing with everything I had, feeling like I was giving all of myself to this one final moment. And then, a relief, a shift, and suddenly... Donovin's head was out.

And then, at exactly 8:26 p.m. on October 27, 2001, the moment that would change my life forever arrived. The first cries of our baby boy, Donovin, echoed through the maternity ward, and I swear, the heavens themselves seemed to open up. In that instant, I felt like the luckiest woman alive. I had no words for what I was feeling — just pure, unfiltered joy.

Donovin weighed eight pounds, sixteen ounces and measured twenty-two inches long. He was perfect, absolutely perfect. My heart swelled with love as I held him in my arms for the first time, so tiny and beautiful. When the nurse handed him to me, he was clean and smelled like a newborn, that special scent that only babies have. His little eyes opened, and in that moment, I was lost in his gaze.

I couldn't help but talk to him, even though I knew I was speaking to a brand-new human being whose comprehension and language skills were nowhere near developed, as I had been led to believe. "Hi, Donovin," I whispered. "It's so nice to meet you. I love you so much, and I'm so proud to be your mom."

And then, in that moment, as if he understood every

word, he wrapped his tiny little hand around my finger. And I cried. I cried harder than I ever had in my life. It wasn't just the joy of meeting him — it was the weight of the responsibility, the love, and the incredible miracle that was my son. I kissed him, over and over again, not wanting to let go.

The moment was magical. It was a moment that no words could ever truly capture. The overwhelming love I felt for Donovin in that moment was beyond anything I had ever known, and it made me think: Could this be the love that God has for us?

Holding him in my arms, I realized that all of the pain, the fear, and the doubts were nothing compared to the love I felt. Donovin, my beautiful boy, was here. And nothing else mattered.

Chapter Seven

Life as Usual

The first few years of Donovin's life felt like a blur. Time seemed to fly, and before I could blink, my tiny newborn had become a curious, adventurous toddler. From the moment he was born, Donovin made parenting feel like a breeze—he was a calm, easygoing baby who rarely cried unless something was wrong. He slept through the night, fed well, and only got fussy when he was hungry or needed a diaper change. The challenge, however, was breastfeeding. Not the act of feeding Donovin itself, but the process of using the breast pump to store milk for when I wasn't around.

I had done my research before becoming a mother, convinced that breastfeeding was the best choice. But as a working mom, I needed to find a way to pump and store milk for when I had to leave Donovin for work. I bought the breast pump with high hopes, armed with a stack of reading material to guide me through the process. I remember sitting in the middle of the bed, reading the instructions, confident that I could manage it.

That confidence quickly evaporated the moment I tried to remove the pump after it was in place. In a panic, I screamed for my mother. She rushed to my side, probably sensing my distress. There I was, one breast still attached to the pump, looking like a hostage, not knowing how to get myself free. Mom, ever the problem-solver, rushed me to the kitchen sink, where she ran warm water over the pump, slowly loosening the suction. I was terrified that I might need to go to the hospital with the pump still attached, but fortunately, the situation was resolved before it got to that point. We both laughed nervously after it was over, but I couldn't help but reflect on how daunting motherhood felt at times, even in these smaller, more humorous moments.

The journey of motherhood, with all its twists and turns, was never what I had expected, but one thing was clear: giving birth to Donovin had been a miraculous experience. I marveled at how some women gave birth without any pain relief at all—no epidural, not even an aspirin. To me, women in general deserved to be celebrated, not only for the act of giving birth but for the lifelong responsibility of nurturing a child.

By January 2002, just a few months after Donovin's birth, my marriage to Malachi was crumbling. The realization hit that we wouldn't grow old together, sipping iced tea on a porch, watching our grandchildren play. We made the difficult decision to separate. With Donovin only three months old, I packed up and moved to Phoenix, Arizona, seeking a fresh start with my son in tow.

The move served a dual purpose. My parents had retired in Arizona and had been living there for a few years, so they would provide a much-needed support system as I navigated this new chapter. More than that, Arizona represented a clean slate—no ties, no past mistakes following me, just the promise of a new beginning for Donovin and me. I had already started applying for jobs before leaving Atlanta, and just days after arriving in Arizona, I had a job interview lined up.

I remember how nervous I was the day of the interview. My dad drove me there since I didn't have a car and didn't know my way around Phoenix yet. I also felt a little ashamed of how I looked—after all, I had packed mostly things for Donovin, not myself. So there I was, sitting in the waiting room wearing an old black maternity skirt (thankfully, no one could tell it was a maternity skirt), flats, and a blouse that barely reached my waist, covering the maternity waistband. I felt out of place sitting next to two well-dressed candidates who looked like they were ready to take on the world. For a moment, I thought about walking out. But as I was about to make my exit, the door opened, and a tall, confident, and graceful woman with salt-and-pepper hair stepped into the room, calling my name.

She introduced herself, leading me into the interview room, where I met two other women, also impeccably dressed, in business suits that screamed professionalism. I felt underdressed and out of place. But as the interview went on, I found myself relaxing. I answered their questions truthfully, even making them laugh a few times. Honestly, I wasn't sure what I was doing there. I didn't have any experience in the field I was applying for, and I had no idea what the job even entailed. It was one of the many interviews I'd gone on after submitting dozens of resumes, and this was the first—and only—employer who had called me back.

After the interview ended, I was told to wait in the lobby. I sat there, my mind spinning, convinced that I hadn't gotten the job. But when they called me back into the room and offered me the position right on the spot, I was stunned. I sat there in disbelief, wondering if someone was going to jump out from behind a curtain and announce that I was on a hidden camera show. But no one did. I couldn't hold back the tears as I accepted the offer. This was it—my fresh start in Phoenix with Donovin.

In the meantime, Donovin was growing and changing at an alarming rate. He went from a tiny baby who couldn't do anything for himself to a curious, independent toddler. He began crawling, then walking, and then talking. His language skills were developing quickly, and soon enough, he was saying things that made us laugh. He would do things that made him seem like an "old soul," like comforting me when I was down.

If he saw that I was upset, he'd come to me, put his tiny arm around me, and say, "Everything is ooookay."

But as fast as Donovin was growing, the chaos of life kept moving just as quickly. There was always something to do, someone to see, and somewhere to go. One day, Donovin somehow managed to escape from his crib. I was sitting quietly, watching television, when I suddenly heard him running down the hall, yelling as if he was leading a parade. He had managed to slip out of his pull-up underwear and was completely naked. When I asked him why he was naked, he just shrugged his tiny shoulders and said, "I don't know." We both laughed, and I ended up carrying him through the house to find his missing underwear.

Donovin was a social butterfly, and I couldn't help but smile at his friendly interactions with everyone. He was a regular at his Pop Pop's house, where his grandfather would take him on little adventures, and his Nana was always there to support him when I was busy. He loved spending time with them, and they loved him right back. My parents were my lifeline, especially as I was navigating life as a single mom.

It was also around this time that Donovin developed a special bond with his father, Malachi. Every Sunday at 3 p.m., Malachi would call to check in with Donovin, and without fail, Donovin would remind me to have my phone ready for his dad's call. Donovin loved talking to Malachi, and Malachi was always grateful that Donovin and I remained civil for his sake.

Kindergarten came around quicker than expected, and Donovin was growing into his own little person. One day, I had to meet with his teacher, Ms. Louise, for a progress check. Donovin, ever the curious and observant child, was sitting in the backseat of the car, nervously asking me not to mention the "song" he had been singing in the car two weeks prior. I couldn't help but laugh when I remembered the incident—he had been singing about "lovely lady lumps," a lyric from a popular song I hadn't even realized he was paying attention to. When I asked him where the "lady lumps" were, he shrugged and said, "I don't know."

At school, Ms. Louise confirmed that Donovin was doing great in kindergarten, and despite his mischievous moments, he was more than ready for first grade. As we finished the meeting, Ms. Louise noticed the storm clouds gathering outside. The Arizona monsoon season had arrived, and we hurried to finish our meeting and get home before the storm hit.

But in that brief moment of reflection, as I watched Donovin continue to grow and thrive, I felt a deep sense of gratitude. Despite the challenges, the unknowns, and the fear of starting over, I was blessed. I had my son, my family, and a new chapter ahead of me. And for that, I was thankful.

This was not my first monsoon season in Phoenix,

Arizona, but the summer of 2004 marked the first monsoon that Donovin could articulate his thoughts about the storm. I'll never forget this particular storm, mainly because Donovin had so much to say about it. For anyone unfamiliar with monsoons, let me offer a brief explanation:

Monsoons are not just about the thunderstorms themselves, but about the larger weather pattern that drives them. The word "monsoon" comes from the Arabic *mausin*, meaning "season" or "wind shift." These seasonal winds bring moisture from the Gulf of Mexico and the Pacific, which, combined with the intense desert heat, leads to a cycle of heavy rainfall, high winds, and sometimes dust storms. But instead of going into a scientific explanation, I'll forever rely on Donovin's simple but accurate description: "It's a very big rain, a lot of wind, and can be just a little bit scary."

On that day, as we drove home, Donovin kept an eye on the sky, repeating that we needed to get inside and lock the doors. I smiled at his serious tone, imagining that he thought the monsoon might try to come inside and steal his toys. I reassured him that we'd be inside long before the storm reached us and there was nothing to fear. He said he wasn't scared, but didn't want to get the car — or us — wet. Whether he was genuinely afraid or just fascinated by the storm, I couldn't tell. But one thing was certain — he was definitely curious.

When we got home, we had just enough time to stand outside and watch the dark clouds roll in. Donovin was quick to say that the storm was coming our way, and he thought it was going to be a big one. As soon as we got inside, the heavy raindrops began to fall, and Donovin exclaimed, "We made it just in time!" We both laughed, realizing it wasn't as dramatic as he had expected, but the rain was definitely coming down hard now.

As we sat together in the living room, listening to the rain pounding against the roof, Donovin asked if I was afraid. I was taken aback by the question and asked, "Why would I be afraid of the rain?" He reassured me, "You shouldn't be afraid, Mom; this is good stuff!" I smiled, feeling comforted by his confidence.

As we settled into our quiet moment, a loud clap of thunder rattled the house, followed by a bright flash of lightning. It was so sudden and intense that I flinched without thinking. I quickly looked at Donovin to see how he was reacting, only to find that he was gripping my hand tightly. His small fingers were so firm it startled me. I tried to smile, reassuring him, but I could tell he was shaken by the thunder. The rain continued, heavy and unrelenting, and Donovin stayed close to me the rest of the evening.

By the time dinner was over and bedtime approached, Donovin informed me that he was going to sleep in my bed because, as he put it, "I don't want you to be afraid." His sweet, thoughtful nature melted my heart. I welcomed him into my bed, and we snuggled together, watching repeats on the Disney Channel. At one point, Donovin turned to me, and it felt like time stopped when he said, "Mom, I love you." I responded, "Baby, I love you more."

We continued to watch TV, but the next burst of thunder was so loud that the power went out. In the sudden darkness, Donovin, ever the problem-solver, asked, "Should we get the candles and flashlights out?" I told him, "Let's just go to sleep now, baby. The TV's sleepy too and has gone to sleep." We lay there in the dark, only the occasional flash of lightning lighting up the room. We listened to the rain and thunder as it continued to drum against the roof and giggled and spoke about everything and nothing. I thanked him for being brave through the storm. Eventually, Donovin fell asleep first, with me still wide awake, listening to the storm and marveling at how close we had become through moments like this.

In the morning, when the storm had passed, Donovin's first words were, "We made it!" And we had. We had weathered the storm together — not just the monsoon outside, but the storm of emotions that came with it. And in that moment, I realized that with Donovin by my side, there was nothing I couldn't face.

Chapter Eight

The Season of Change

In June 2005, Donovin was just four months shy of his fourth birthday. Another monsoon season was upon us in Phoenix, Arizona, but this time Donovin didn't have much to say about the impending storms. His mind was occupied with something far more exciting: his upcoming trip to Disneyland. While he couldn't fully grasp the enormity of Disneyland, I made sure to show him videos and talk about the trip. He was a little confused but mostly excited.

Things were going well for both of us. Donovin was thriving in preschool, and I was working on my master's degree. He spent a lot of time with his Pop Pop and Nana, which was a relief because I knew he was safe and well cared for. My only concern was how much I missed him, especially on nights when he stayed at Pop Pop and Nana's, and I was tied up in class late into the evening.

When we did have time together, Donovin and I would often wind down by laying in bed, eating popcorn, and watching movies — many of which he had seen a hundred times before. But on other nights, we would just talk. He'd tell me about his day, and I'd listen, while I carefully filtered what I shared. My work in government meant that there were topics I couldn't expose him to yet. During one of these conversations, Donovin told me that Nana had explained I was going to school at night to give him a better life. He asked me to explain what that meant.

I smiled and confirmed that Nana was right. I wanted him to understand how important education is, how it would give him choices in life, and how it would help him become whoever he wanted to be. Donovin thought for a moment, then looked at me and said, "Mom, you don't want me to be stupid. You want me to be smart!"

I was stunned by his simple yet profound observation. Donovin, you are correct, I don't want you to be stupid. I want you to be smart — and do better than me," I told him. He grinned and replied, "Okay, I will!"

It was moments like these that made me realize how quickly my little boy was growing up.

On May 27, 2005, Malachi called me at work, which I did not realized at the time would be our last conversation, to let me know he was going out of town for the Memorial Day weekend and his birthday on June 1st. He told me he wouldn't be able to call Donovin during their regular Sunday 3:00 pm call but would instead call him on Tuesday, May 31st, at 6:30 pm. We talked about how Donovin was doing, how proud Malachi was of him, and how thankful I was for the pictures he had sent of himself for Donovin to have. We spoke at length, and for the first time in a long while, I felt a sense of peace between us.

It was a strange, bittersweet feeling — knowing that Malachi and I could never be together again as husband and wife, but still shared love and respect for each other. When he told me he was proud of how I was raising Donovin, I could barely hold back tears. I thanked him and reminded him that I would always love him because he was Donovin's father. He paused for a moment before responding, his voice thick with emotion: "I love you too, and I always will."

We ended our call with words of love and mutual understanding, but something in his tone made me uneasy. He asked me to take care of Donovin and to make sure he knew who his father was. I didn't understand why he'd say that after almost four years of regular contact. I asked him to clarify, and Malachi repeated the request. It lingered in my mind as I hung up the phone.

The next morning, on May 28th, Malachi's sister called me. Her voice was shaky, though controlled, and I immediately sensed something was wrong. She told me that Malachi had been found unconscious in his hotel room while on vacation. He was on life support. She said she would keep me updated and headed to the hospital to be by his side.

I stood frozen for a moment, trying to process what she'd said, then walked into Donovin's room. He was asleep, blissfully unaware of the storm that was brewing in my heart. I watched him sleep for a while, wondering how I was going to explain this to him when the time came.

I had always been open with Donovin, always honest. Even as an infant, I spoke to him as though he were older than his age. He was the kind of child who would hear something, then come to me with questions. And I would answer him directly, without sugarcoating things. As I prepared breakfast that morning, I considered what to say to him. But I decided it was best to wait for an update before I said anything.

Donovin woke up as usual, cheerful and full of energy. After breakfast, we went to the park, then planned to stop by one of his favorite stores where I would allow him to pick two items that I would purchase for him. The excitement in his eyes was infectious, and I couldn't help but smile as I watched him play with his friends at the park. Meanwhile, I struggled to hide the sadness creeping in, the weight of uncertainty gnawing at me as I thought about Malachi.

After some time, I reminded Donovin about our trip to the store, and he was quick to wash his hands and rush to the car, ready for his reward. We drove to the store, and I could hear the excitement in his voice when he saw the familiar building. I loved how something as small as a trip to the dollar store could bring him so much joy, but then again, he knew he would walk out with valuable loot.

As usual, I confirmed the deal: he could pick two toys if he behaved. He eagerly ran to the toy section, examining everything with care, as if deciding which two toys would be worthy of taking home that day. He came back to me with a huge grin, showing off his picks — his two carefully selected treasures.

We hadn't been home long when Malachi's sister called again. This time, her tone was softer, tinged with sadness. She informed me that Malachi had suffered a brain aneurysm and was not expected to survive. While I was aware of what a brain aneurysm was, for clarification and details, I had to Google what a brain aneurysm was. When I understood the severity, my heart sank. I felt like the ground had disappeared beneath me.

I called my mom, tears flooding my eyes, and shared the devastating news. Donovin must have sensed something was wrong, as he was quietly and unusually following me around the house. He watched me, his big brown eyes full of concern, and eventually he asked why I was crying. I didn't know how to answer him, sure it would be with complete honesty, but how do I start this particular conversation? I decided that I would have this discussion with Donovin tomorrow, this would give me time to decide on how I would tell him.

May 29, 2005, was a blur of emotions. That evening, as

I sat in my oversized chair in my home, staring out the large panoramic window at the sunset, Malachi's sister called again. She informed me that Malachi had been declared brain-dead, and his life support would be disconnected. I struggled to hold it together as I listened, but when the call ended, the dam broke and the flood of emotions was released. The cry that escaped me was raw, followed by a gut-wrenching sob that felt like it would never end.

I called my mom again, and as always, she offered to come over as support, but this time I told her I just wanted to be alone with Donovin. She understood.

When Malachi passed, I knew I would have to explain it to Donovin, but I was having a hard enough time processing it myself. He and I had just spoken days earlier, and now, out of nowhere, he was gone.

As I sat in the chair, still in shock, Donovin came into the room holding one of his new toys. He climbed into my lap, resting his head on my chest, and told me softly, "It's going to be oooookay." His sweet, innocent assurance only made me cry harder, and I held him tighter, feeling his warmth and comfort. We sat there for what felt like hours, until the phone rang again. This time, I received the final confirmation: Malachi was gone.

I didn't cry during that phone call. Instead, I felt a deep sadness for Malachi's sister, who had to make one of the hardest decisions of her life. I asked her how she was holding up, and she assured me she would be okay. I was amazed at what I perceived to be her strength, because I felt completely broken.

Still cradling Donovin, who was sitting quietly on my lap, I finally knew it was time to explain the situation to him. I asked him to remember our talks about God and heaven. He listened intently, his eyes wide with understanding.

I had often said that Donovin, at three years old, seemed to have the soul of a much older person, and that day, he proved it. As I started to speak, he stopped me and asked, "Mom, why are you sad? Is it because of heaven?"

I kissed his forehead, gathering strength from his wisdom. "I'm not sad about heaven, baby. I'm sad because your daddy went to heaven."

He looked up at the sky, through that same large panoramic window, then turned back to me, with a gentle smile on his face. "My dad is behind those clouds, and he can still see me."

His words were simple, but they brought me unimaginable peace. "He's okay, Mom, he's with God" he added, hugging me tight. "We'll be okay."

In that moment, I realized that Donovin's faith and innocence were more than I could have ever asked for or even imagine. Through his pure heart, he reminded me as we both sat there, now quietly watching the sunset, that even in the sadness, there was beauty, and there was God.

When Donovin turned four years old on October 27, 2005, as planned, family and friends celebrated his birthday at Disneyland. Those few days at the park were truly magical, and it seemed that Donovin and I had managed to put the weight of the previous four months behind us. We often talked about Malachi, and I shared with Donovin, whenever he asked, that I missed his dad. Donovin, in turn, would tell me that he, too, missed talking to his dad, but sometimes he would talk to the sky so his dad could hear him.

Shortly after Malachi's death, I began therapy. Although I had a strong support system around me, I felt alone, scared, and helpless. As a psychology major, I struggled to find a therapist I could connect with. I knew what their training involved and what they would try to get me to acknowledge: that I was looking for someone to listen, not someone to "fix" me. I went through four therapists before I found one who understood this. She was a petite, soft-spoken Caucasian woman, always dressed in neutral colors, never too fancy. She didn't ask me the usual open-ended questions designed to get me to reveal my thoughts and feelings. Instead, she simply listened. And then, one day, she identified a fear I didn't even know I had — a fear related to Donovin.

She asked if I'd be open to bringing Donovin in for a session. I immediately agreed.

When I took Donovin to therapy with me, I told him we were going to see a nice lady because Mom was feeling sad. In true Donovin fashion, he simply replied, "Sure!" When we arrived, I noticed he had a habit I share: sizing up his surroundings. He knew not to touch anything, but he walked around the room looking at everything, glancing back at me to check for approval. I approved.

I introduced Donovin to the therapist, and he smiled and said hello. She asked him if he liked to draw, and he looked at me as if to say, *Didn't you tell her I'm three, of course I like to draw?* Then, he turned back to her and answered, "Yes." She handed him several sheets of clean, white paper and a box of crayons.

Before he started drawing, the therapist asked Donovin how he felt about his dad dying. Donovin took a crayon in each hand, looked at her, and stated matter-of-factly, "My dad is in heaven with God, and he's doing good." I watched her expression as she processed what he had just said. She glanced at me, and I thought, *well, this is either going to make or break her career.*

She asked him if he would be willing to draw a picture of his dad. Donovin, who appeared to be deep in thought over his impending masterpiece, looked up at her and said, "Sure." I stepped in, reminding him that he could go ahead and start, knowing that without a direct prompt, Donovin might not begin at all. The therapist had asked if he *would* draw, but Donovin needed the certainty of being told *to* draw. I learned this early on — with Donovin, you had to be direct.

After only a few minutes, Donovin announced that he was finished. The therapist asked to see his drawing. As she handed it to me, I stared at it for a moment before turning to Donovin and asking him to explain his work.

He walked over to stand between the therapist and me, and I handed him his drawing. He began explaining it, starting on the left side of the paper where he had drawn me in a dress and him in shorts. We were both walking with smiles on our faces. In the center of the drawing was his dad, also in shorts, smiling and singing. Donovin explained that his dad was singing a happy song. Directly above his dad, he had drawn a bright orange sun with a smiley face, and on the right side of the paper, he had written the word "haven," which he explained was *heaven*—with an arrow pointing to his dad.

I smiled and praised him for his drawing, and Donovin beamed. He turned to the therapist, who was still processing his picture, and she finally spoke, telling Donovin that his drawing was wonderful and that everyone in it looked incredibly happy. Donovin simply nodded, confirming that everyone in the drawing was happy.

I was flooded with relief. Any fears I had about Donovin struggling emotionally or holding onto any unresolved grief evaporated in that moment. The therapist, too, seemed impressed by how Donovin expressed himself so clearly. She had picked up on the fact that Donovin would not have drawn anything without a direct prompt, and yet his ability to show his emotions through art was profound. She even expressed amazement at how clearly, he communicated his feelings for his father.

As Donovin returned to his drawing, I watched him, my heart swelling with pride. Tears came to my eyes, not from sadness, but from the incredible strength I saw in him. He was not just a child; he was a little person with a depth of understanding far beyond his years.

Later that day, as we made our way into Disneyland with Pop Pop, Nana, and our family friend LaMetra (whom we affectionately called Meta), it was unclear whether Donovin had any idea of the excitement that awaited him. We went first to the visitor's center to register Donovin's birthday. He received a special birthday badge with his name and age written on it, which he proudly wore. Now and then, he'd glance down at it to make sure it was still there.

Then, he was invited to take a call from Tiger on a giant, colorful rotary phone designed by Disney himself. Donovin, who was always a little skeptical of anything that wasn't entirely real to him, reluctantly took the phone. As he sat up on the counter, holding the oversized receiver, he answered the call with an air of mild disinterest. When the call ended, he looked at all of us and, in his usual deadpan way, said, "You know he's not real, right?" We all exchanged amused glances, and I thought to myself, *Well, Donovin is certainly four now—he's got that straight-shooter thing down.*

As we took the train to the other side of the park, Donovin seemed overwhelmed by all the new sights, sounds, and smells. People would stop to wish him a happy birthday, and at first, he seemed puzzled as to how these strangers knew. But within minutes, he looked down at his badge and smiled. It was then that I realized he had figured it out—his badge was the reason everyone knew it was his special day.

We rode the Dumbo ride together, and Donovin simply enjoyed the experience. I found joy in watching him take in the moment. During *Pirates of the Caribbean*, Donovin was mesmerized by the music, the action, and the dancing characters. His eyes darted from one scene to the next, and I couldn't help but feel like the luckiest mother in the world, able to witness his excitement.

When we went on the Haunted Mansion ride, Donovin initially wasn't too keen on it. His little hands grasped mine tightly, signaling that he was uneasy. I picked him up and held him close until we got to the actual ride. Once seated, Donovin nestled as close to me as possible, and I reassured him that everything would be okay. He relaxed, and we rode together through the eerie, spooky mansion.

That day, surrounded by the joy of Disneyland, I found solace in the fact that, despite all the heartbreak we had endured, Donovin was finding his own ways to heal, to process, and to grow.

By the time we were ready to eat, Donovin was exhausted, so I rented a stroller for him to rest in. He eventually drifted off to sleep, Mickey Mouse hat perched on his head. As he sat there, munching on his snacks, he took in all the wonders of Disneyland, his little eyes wide with curiosity. We stayed well into the evening so that Donovin could experience the Electrical Parade, a tradition that, as a child and well into my teenage years, I had come to love. Even now, as an adult, I can still hear that electric-sounding music that signaled the parade had started, winding its way down Main Street. My mom later told me that Donovin was fascinated by Tinker Bell, especially how she was able to fly. There was something at Disneyland, after all, that even Donovin — now also known as Hercules Poirot — couldn't figure out.

The most memorable part of Donovin's fourth birthday at Disneyland came at the end of our visit. While there were countless magical moments, it was this one that stood out: Donovin and his Pop Pop went to ride the train one last time, and somehow, they ended up standing alone on the platform with Mickey Mouse. Just the three of them. No other children, adults, or characters in sight. For what seemed like an eternity, Donovin and Mickey Mouse spent quality time together. Donovin was overjoyed, grinning from ear to ear as we snapped pictures of this rare moment. Later, when Donovin recounted his experience, he simply said, "Mom, that was Mickey Mouse!" He had gone from being a serious, mature little boy to a child once more, fully embracing the magic of the moment.

October 2005 also marked Donovin's first Halloween where he was old enough to participate. Although I wasn't particularly fond of the holiday, I wanted Donovin to have the same experience I had growing up — with one big difference: I was determined to explain the holiday to him. I wasn't on a high horse about it, but I felt that Donovin deserved to understand what Halloween was all about. Some might ask why I felt the need to explain a holiday to a four-year-old, and the answer is simple: Donovin wasn't your typical four-year-old. He asked a lot of questions, and I believed in giving him honest answers. While I, of course, tried to shield him from certain harsh realities, if he asked about something, I gave him the truth. He never once expected to be treated like a baby. In fact, he often made it clear, even at age three, that certain things were for babies, and he wasn't one.

One day, Donovin informed me that he wasn't black, but actually brown, and he took the time to show me the difference using his crayons. How could I argue with the truth, even if it came from a three-year-old? I couldn't. Donovin decided he wanted to dress up for Halloween as Tigger from *Winnie the Pooh*. So, we found a Tigger costume, and on October 31, 2005, Donovin collected candy as Tigger, thoroughly enjoying his first Halloween.

When November rolled around, we celebrated Thanksgiving. Donovin loved to eat, no matter the occasion, but especially on Thanksgiving. My mom (Nana) always went all out, decorating the house and preparing a semi-formal dinner at the dining room table, complete with the good china.

During this time, Donovin became captivated by *The Wiggles*, a children's music group from Australia. He loved watching their shows on TV, and he had nearly every Wiggles toy and DVD. He even picked up on their accents, standing in front of the TV, singing along to their songs. His favorite Wiggle was Murray, the Red Wiggle. Donovin never told me why Murray was his favorite, but there was no need for an explanation — it just was.

When I found out *The Wiggles* were coming to the Dodge Theater in downtown Phoenix, I knew I couldn't let Donovin miss it. So, as soon as tickets became available, I bought them. Nana joined us for the concert, and as we walked toward the theater, Donovin, with his usual sense of authority, led the way. I asked him to stop for a picture in front of the theater, next to the poster of *The Wiggles*, and he complied without a fuss.

At the concert, many of the other children jumped out of their seats as soon as the music started. It reminded me of my own excitement at my first Sade concert, when I couldn't help but jump up and cheer along with the crowd. But Donovin, the observer, sat quietly, taking in the performance. Then, he spotted Murray on stage. His face lit up, and he turned to me, whispering, "That's Murray!" His whole demeanor shifted, and he became more animated, clapping and cheering as he watched his favorite Wiggle perform.

During the intermission, Donovin shared his excitement with me, making sure I knew that the people on stage were the real *The Wiggles*. He was in awe of the entire experience. As the final stage of the concert unfolded, nearly all the children were up on their feet, dancing and singing along. But Donovin remained seated, eyes glued to the stage with an intensity I had never seen before.

I glanced at him, wanting to gauge his excitement. His expression was a mix of joy, amazement, and a hint of disbelief. His eyes were locked on the performance, and then, suddenly, it happened: Murray, the Red Wiggle, was right in front of him, singing and dancing directly to him. Donovin, in complete shock, finally broke into the widest grin I had ever seen. It was as if he had met his hero in person, and for him, everything was perfect.

Donovin would go on to attend other concerts, including performances by *Bear in the Big Blue House* and *Elmo and Friends*, but the day he saw Murray live in concert was the one he would never forget. It was a moment of pure, unadulterated joy.

Christmas 2005 brought even more excitement. Donovin was now at an age where he could really get into the magic of Christmas — the lights, the sounds, the smells, and, yes, the excitement of Santa Claus. But first, we had to go shopping for the outfit Donovin would wear to his preschool holiday show. I never thought shopping with a four-year-old boy would be such an ordeal, but it was. I had told him we needed to get a pair of pants, a shirt, and a sweater, and he agreed. We quickly found the pants — dark blue jeans — and the sweater, a perfect match for the pants, with red and beige stripes across the chest.

The real challenge came when it was time to pick a shirt. Donovin held up every possible shirt that might match the sweater, turning it over and holding it up to his body, then discarding it with a firm "No!" He couldn't settle on anything, and it seemed as though the decision-making process was taking forever. By the time he decided to go with just an undershirt, I was more than ready to move on. The shoes, thankfully, were easy to pick — beige loafers that matched the sweater perfectly. Donovin was finally ready to perform in his first school Christmas production.

As we were leaving the shopping center, I asked Donovin if he wanted to meet Santa. He agreed, though I could tell he wasn't exactly enthusiastic. There was a short line, and I assumed that most kids had already met Santa, so I thought nothing of it. But when I got a good look at Santa, I quickly realized there was something off. This Santa was unnervingly thin, pale, and wearing cowboy boots that looked like they had seen better days. The moment I made eye contact with him, a chill ran down my spine. Donovin, ever perceptive, squeezed my hand and announced he was ready to go home. I didn't ask him why he didn't want to meet Santa; at that point, I didn't want him to either.

On the drive home, Donovin suddenly brought up Santa and matter-of-factly informed me that the man we had just seen was *not* Santa. He insisted that this person needed to be reported for trying to act like Santa when, clearly, he wasn't. I was inclined to agree, not just because of his odd appearance but also because of the unsettling vibe I got when our eyes met. There was just something off about that Santa impostor. Later that day, I called the shopping center to file a complaint about

Santa's less-than-ideal performance, and although the lady on the phone seemed genuinely interested in my report, I never knew if anything came of it.

That Christmas season was filled with so much joy and wonder. I was absolutely the proudest parent in the audience at Donovin's preschool holiday show, and I made sure to capture every moment on video, clapping louder than anyone else. There he was—my little boy, standing on stage in his dark blue ash-colored jeans, his dark blue sweater with the red and beige stripes, and his perfectly chosen beige loafers. He looked so grown up, singing along with his classmates. My heart swelled when I saw that Donovin had spotted his Nana and Pop Pop in the crowd. His face lit up, and he flashed a quick smile at them before turning back to the stage with renewed focus.

After the show, Donovin asked me, with a serious tone, whether I thought his performance was better than "Nadia." I was momentarily confused, until his excitement exploded: "Nadia, The Lion, the Witch, and the Wardrobe!" It clicked—Donovin was comparing his preschool debut to his recent trip to the movies. In early December 2005, Donovin saw his first film at the theater—*The Chronicles of Narnia: The Lion, the Witch and the Wardrobe*. With wide eyes and a look of pure awe, he had been mesmerized by the big screen. That moment left a mark on his memory, one he clearly carried with him.

At the stoplight, I turned to smile at him and told him that I loved his performance far more than the movie. He grinned back at me, that sweet, heartwarming smile that never failed to brighten my day. "I love you, Mom," he said, his little voice carrying so much sincerity that I couldn't help but feel a wave of love wash over me. I met his gaze through the rearview mirror and, with a lump in my throat, replied, "I love you too, Donovin."

One of the most memorable mornings was when Donovin woke up early and snuck into my bed. I could feel his smile before I even opened my eyes. When I asked him how he got there, his answer was pure Donovin logic: "I walked from my room into your room and got in the bed!" And then he laughed—one of those infectious laughs that made me laugh too. That day, we stayed home with no real plans other than to bake cookies, watch a movie, and put up our Christmas tree. But Donovin had other ideas—he insisted on changing the music from Ray Charles to Christmas tunes and invited me to dance with him. We spun around the living room, laughing and dancing, until we both agreed it was time to get serious about making our cookies.

Christmas Day 2005 was, of course, a magical day. We spent the night at my parents' house, eager to experience Donovin's first Christmas where he truly understood the excitement of gifts under the tree. I had never seen him quite so stunned. As he looked at all the gifts that had appeared overnight, it was almost as if he didn't know how to process the abundance. But when Nana and Pop Pop joined in and handed him his first gift, the joy on his face was priceless. The excitement built with every gift he opened.

Among his many gifts, one stood out—Uncle Chuck and Aunt Dot had given him a children's Bible. Donovin was not yet old enough to read, but that didn't stop him from asking me to read it to him, front to back, over and over. I read him that Bible a million times, and every time we reached Psalm 23:5, he would giggle at the words, "You anoint my head with oil." He would laugh and ask, "Is it hot oil?" Of course, we would both laugh together, and I'd explain that it wasn't, but Donovin loved our special time. He loved the comfort of snuggling up in bed with me, listening to me read his favorite stories.

As we rang in the New Year in January 2006, we didn't stay up late. Instead, we toasted with apple juice and cookies— just the two of us. I read him his Bible, and we talked about how much we loved each other. It was a quiet, intimate moment that felt just perfect for the start of a new year.

By February 2006, Arizona's "cruel winter weather" had settled in, though anyone from a colder climate would find our temperatures in the mid-50s a bit laughable. Still, Donovin and I embraced it, bundled up on the occasional rainy days and enjoying our time indoors.

On Valentine's Day, Donovin asked if I would be his Valentine. When I asked him what he knew about the holiday, he simply said, "It's about love, and I love you." I couldn't help but giggle, and asked him if he only loved me on that day. He giggled and replied, "No, I love you every day, but I extra love you today!" His thoughtfulness and charm never ceased to amaze me.

With the help of his Nana, Donovin presented me with a stuffed bear, some candy, and a red plastic rose with a little balloon attached that read, *Happy Valentine's Day, Mom.* He stood there, waiting for my reaction. When he saw the joy on my face, his smile widened, and I felt as though my heart might burst with love for him.

Then, on February 17, 2006, I woke up to find Donovin had snuck into my bed again. His smile was the first thing I saw, and as he asked me to read his Bible, I could tell something wasn't quite right. As I read, I noticed he was having trouble breathing, and soon he started coughing. There was no fever, but something felt off. He admitted that he wasn't feeling well and wanted to sleep.

A little uneasy, I dressed him and took him to see his doctor. Without an appointment, she still managed to see him right away. I never forgot the fear that flashed in her eyes when she told me that Donovin needed to be transported by ambulance to the Emergency Room. She said Donovin had pneumonia, one lung completely inflamed, the other partially so. It didn't make sense—he had been his normal, energetic self until that morning.

Though confused and scared, I remained calm for Donovin's sake. I explained the situation to him, assuring him that the ambulance ride was just to help him feel better, and that I'd be right behind. He was completely unfazed, even smiling at the paramedics. "Okay, Mom!" he said.

As I followed the ambulance to the hospital, I couldn't hold back my tears any longer. I called my mom, who reminded me to stay focused and drive safely.

That night, as I sat beside Donovin's bed in the Intensive Care Unit, I looked at him peacefully sleeping, tubes in place, and thought about how quickly everything had changed. One moment we were baking cookies and enjoying Christmas, and the next, I was in a hospital room, praying for his recovery. Donovin, however, took it all in stride. He had a bravery beyond his years, and in the midst of the fear, he remained calm, never once showing the anxiety that I felt deep inside.

How was any of this possible? Just hours ago, we were at home, laughing, watching *The Suite Life of Zack & Cody*, enjoying the simplicity of a normal day. We were so carefree, so full of joy, and now, I was face-to-face with doctors who assured me that Donovin's illness was nothing out of the ordinary. They said it was something they'd seen and treated countless times before. I even remember one doctor telling me not to worry.

I found that advice both strange and infuriating. *Donovin is my child,* I thought. *He is in crisis, and I am powerless to help him.* Telling me not to worry was like telling me not to breathe. It was an impossible request.

Ultimately, Donovin was in the hospital for weeks. His condition worsened, and they moved him from a regular room to the ICU. They found an infection in one of his lungs, and the best course of action, they said, was surgery to remove the infection. When the doctor explained that he would need surgery, I felt my heart drop into my stomach. The thought of my four-year-old undergoing surgery was too much to bear. My mind raced, but what struck me the most was the overwhelming fear and sadness I felt.

At that time, my walk with God wasn't what it is now. I was that person who only called on God when I needed something. After a difficult church experience in Atlanta, I'd abandoned my search for God in organized religion, dismissing both church and its people as fake. So, at this moment, I prayed to God — though I'm not sure what exactly I said. I remember thinking, *God is probably asking, "Who is this?"*

On February 20, 2006, Donovin's surgery was scheduled for 1:00 p.m. Before the procedure, he and I talked about what he wanted to eat once he was able to eat solid food again. He said, "I want Coke and chips and salsa," and I promised him that when he was able, he could have as much of both as he wanted.

Looking back on that moment, my heart is heavy with emotion. Donovin seemed to be extra loving that day, more so than usual, if that's even possible. He took his time hugging everyone before heading into the operating room, but our moment together felt especially meaningful. He hugged me tightly, then extended his arms to show me how much he loved me. I mirrored his gesture, extending my arms back, and he said, "That sure is a lot of love." We both smiled.

He asked, "Will you come back with me and the doctors?" and I told him, "No, baby, I can't go with you." Then he asked the question that broke my heart: "So I have to be brave?" My answer was simple: "Yes, baby, you have to be brave."

We shared one final smile before he was wheeled away.

As the group gathered in the hospital waiting room, I felt an inexplicable unease. Something in my spirit knew something was wrong, but I couldn't place it. When everyone went downstairs to the cafeteria to eat, I decided to stay behind. I hadn't eaten in over 24 hours, fasting alongside

Donovin for his surgery.

Then, I saw one of Donovin's nurses, Gina, leaving the cafeteria. She looked at me, but the moment our eyes met, she turned and hurriedly left. Her expression — a mixture of sadness and fear — sent a jolt of panic through me. I turned to my mom, saying, "Something's wrong." My mom, ever the calming presence, reassured me that everything was fine, but my maternal instincts screamed that something wasn't right. I needed to get back upstairs.

Once we returned to Donovin's room, another nurse instructed us to go to a small, unused office space. The moment we walked into that room, I knew. *This is bad. Something is very wrong.*

We waited in that room for what felt like hours, though it was only about ten minutes. When they finally led us to another room, my heart sank. I could see the doctors already gathered, and I immediately locked eyes with Gina. She couldn't meet my gaze, and her red, swollen eyes told me everything. She had been crying.

I was numb as I absorbed the sight of the doctors, their faces grim. The world seemed to move in slow motion as I tried to process what was happening. And then, one of the doctors spoke. "I'm sorry."

Sorry for what? What was he apologizing for? I barely registered the rest of his words, my mind reeling. I heard someone from the group cry out, "No!" But why? Why were they saying *no*?

Then another doctor, his head down, spoke quietly, "We did everything we could, but it was a blood clot. We didn't even start the surgery."

Gina's cry pierced the air. It was a sound that rattled my soul and echoed through the room. Another doctor added, "He was asleep when he passed. He wasn't in any pain."

For a split second, I couldn't breathe. My body went cold as what was happening slowly started to sink in, but my mind rejected it. *This can't be real.* I wanted to scream at them. I wanted to shout, *Liar!* But my body had already betrayed me. My legs went weak, and I collapsed, crumpling to the floor. I couldn't process it. I couldn't breathe. The pain in my chest was a force I can't describe, as if I had been hit by a truck — or perhaps something worse.

The shock was immediate. The air left my lungs. The floor felt as though it had disappeared beneath me. The overwhelming pain — it was physical, emotional, spiritual, all at once. It hit me with the intensity of an accident, and I felt like I was sinking into the ground, broken and lost.

Donovin was gone. My little boy, my heart, my world — gone.

At 1:25 p.m. on February 20, 2006, Donovin Malachi Stokes passed away at St. Joseph's Hospital in Phoenix,

Arizona. I was numb. Broken. Inconsolable. And angry. Angry at the doctors, at the universe, at God.

Where was this God I thought I'd been searching for? Where was He now?

Chapter Nine

Heartbreak in Motion

Donovin is no longer here. The sun is up, and the date has changed, but Donovin is no longer here. The birds are chirping, but Donovin is no longer here. The wind is blowing, but Donovin is no longer here. People are outside moving about with their new day, but Donovin is no longer here.

Why is everyone and everything acting like Donovin was never really here? Why are people still eating, smiling, talking, and enjoying life? Why is the world still rotating? Donovin is no longer here!

There I was, sleep-deprived, sad, angry at the world, and feeling an overwhelming level of mourning and grief, yet I found myself sitting in a doctor's office. I knew that because of my array of emotions, I was having an anxiety attack mixed with a serious level of depression and sleep deprivation. My body felt like it was betraying me, no longer capable of functioning in any meaningful way. Yet here I was, being asked questions I couldn't even begin to answer, because I was struggling with thinking, let alone comprehending anything.

Then she entered the exam room, a doctor I had never seen before, sharing her medical wisdom. Based on our brief conversations about how I was feeling, she was convinced I was having a heart attack. At one point while I was sitting there, listening to her somewhat panicked over how high my blood pressure was, expressing concern that I was on the brink of something catastrophic, I found myself giggling. It was a strange, almost disorienting reaction, fueled by the exhaustion that weighed on my entire being — like the last flicker of a dying lightbulb.

In the midst of this chaos, the giggle was an odd, fleeting moment of release. It wasn't from humor, but from sheer fatigue, like when your body runs on empty but somehow still manages to power through. The absurdity of the situation hit me. Here I was, listening to this doctor, and for a split second, I thought my four-year psychology degree might actually qualify me to diagnose myself — though of course, that wasn't the case. I know what's wrong with me, it's not a heart attack, I thought, but I kept my silence, listening as the doctor continued.

She asked why my blood pressure was so high. You see, I had never had high blood pressure before — it had always been normal. But now, it was dangerously high, and I could see her growing more concerned by the second.

I looked at her — this mature, no-nonsense doctor with short brown hair, a bit too severe for my liking, but with an air of care I couldn't ignore. She reminded me of my high school gym teacher — a tough woman who wasn't afraid to shout orders and yet, underneath that hard exterior, had a heart full of compassion. I could still remember that day in gym class when a student had been hit in the face with a fast-moving basketball. The poor girl had collapsed to the floor, dazed and in pain. Our gym teacher had reacted quickly, rushing to her side, removing her own sweater to cushion the girl's head. It was a simple, kind gesture, and I remembered feeling relieved that someone was there who truly cared — not just to follow protocol, but to care.

In that moment, sitting in the doctor's office, I found myself thinking of that gym teacher again. And here, in this sterile, white-walled room, I was being treated with a similar compassion, as this doctor showed genuine concern for me, even as I sat there unable to fully grasp what was happening to my body. My own body was betraying me, and I felt lost, as if I had forgotten how to care for myself. I could barely eat, and I didn't even know when I last took a shower. The thought of it seemed too exhausting, too impossible.

Still, the doctor's question hung in the air. "Why is your blood pressure so high?" I looked at her, as if trying to figure out how to answer. Finally, my voice, weak and shaky, broke through the silence. "My son died yesterday."

The words felt foreign as they escaped my lips. My son died yesterday. Saying them out loud again was like reopening a wound that I hadn't even realized was still gaping. The doctor paused, and I saw something shift in her face. Her demeanor softened, and she asked if I needed to speak with someone about Donovin's death. I could feel the heaviness in my chest, the ache that no words could truly touch. In that moment, all I wanted was to sleep.

Just sleep. Please, just let me sleep.

I wanted to tell her that I didn't need a therapist, that I didn't need someone to listen to me. I just needed rest. But deep down, I knew that I would eventually need to talk about Donovin, though I wasn't ready for it yet. Not now.

"I just need to sleep," I told her, my voice small, almost defeated.

Her concern was palpable. She suggested that I undergo an EKG to rule out any heart damage, just in case I was, in fact, having a heart attack.

Laying there, waiting for the EKG to be hooked up, I couldn't help but wonder: Can an EKG detect a broken heart? Could it somehow read the grief that was taking over my body, heart, and mind? I thought about Donovin, who had just been with me the day before — and now he was gone. Was there any medication that could fix this overwhelming, never-ending sadness? Was there a way to fill the gaping hole in my chest, the one that was so deep and raw, it felt like I might never breathe again?

As I lay there, I thought that if I were having a heart

attack, maybe I could just close my eyes and fade away. At least, then, the pain would stop, at least then, I would be in peace, at least then, I would be with Donovin. The emotional exhaustion was so intense that I didn't care whether I lived or died. I just wanted it to end, to stop feeling this tired. Mentally and emotionally tired.

The bittersweet news was that the EKG confirmed I wasn't having a heart attack. My heart wasn't physically damaged. The doctors said I had something called "stress cardiomyopathy," also known as broken heart syndrome. It seemed fitting, in a way, as if my body had reacted to the loss of Donovin in the only way it knew how. My heart, the very thing that had kept me alive, was now bruised, fragile, and cracking under the weight of grief.

I left the hospital that day with a prescription for sleeping pills, high blood pressure medication, and a diagnosis that was as unexpected as it was heartbreaking. Broken heart syndrome — a term that felt too real, too close to home.

That night, when I finally made it back to the place where Donovin had lived, laughed, and loved, the emptiness was unbearable. The world had kept moving, as it always does, but I was stuck. Stuck in a place where nothing made sense. And all I could think was, how can the world keep going when mine has come to a screeching halt?

As I sat in the quiet of my home, every corner seemed to echo with the absence of Donovin. His toys, his clothes, his little shoes — all left behind like remnants of a life that had been taken too soon. My fingers instinctively reached for the small blanket that had been draped across his bed, but the emptiness it held only made the silence feel louder.

I wanted to scream, to shake the world awake, to make them understand that *he was here*. But what good would it do? No one could bring him back. The world had moved on, as it always does. And here I was, stuck in the past, desperate to hold onto memories that were slipping away like sand through my fingers.

Chapter Ten

The Funeral

Leading up to the funeral, there was a constant buzz—people coming and going, phone calls, the doorbell ringing, and packages piling up like an endless stream. For a moment, I thought UPS and the United States Postal Service had set up a satellite office at my parent's house. I received word about who had already arrived from out of town and who was still enroute. People were showing up at my parents' home, each one a reminder of the far-reaching impact Donovin had on the lives of those around him.

Among all the chaos, the constant stream of visitors, and the flurry of activities, there were two things that stuck with me in those moments. The first was the overwhelming love, pouring in from both near and far. Family and friends circled around me, never pushing for conversation or forcing meaningless chatter. On the rare occasion that they spoke, it was simply to offer a word of comfort, to sit quietly with me, or to hold space for my grief. It might have seemed to them like they weren't doing much, but to me, their presence was a silent, steadfast support. Their simple act of being there—without asking for anything in return—felt like a warm blanket wrapping around me in the coldest, most vulnerable time of my life.

The second moment that stands out in my memory is one that, on the surface, seemed almost trivial, but in its depth, it was nothing short of a divine intervention. The night before the funeral, my sister Janeen, along with a handful of family members—including my dear friend LaMetra—ended up in my room for what can only be described as a massive sleepover. Amidst the late-night quiet and the surreal exhaustion of the preceding days, LaMetra, in her infinite wisdom, made me laugh hysterically when she jokingly offered to spoon with me to help me sleep. In that moment, I felt a flash of peace—a brief reprieve from the heavy weight of grief that had consumed me. It was one of those moments that only God could have orchestrated—comfort and laughter, wrapped together in a beautiful, unexpected package.

The day of Donovin's funeral was one of the brightest and sunniest days on record for the Phoenix Metropolitan area. The clear, crisp air and the endless blue sky seemed almost out of place, as if nature itself were out of sync with the tragedy unfolding below. Donovin had always loved the color blue, and so the funeral home was adorned in his favorite hue— baby blue linens, ribbons, and flowers—reminding me of the vibrancy of his spirit, now gone. It felt, for a brief moment, as though heaven itself was preparing to receive him, making the earthly sorrow a little more bearable.

Arriving at the funeral home, the surreal reality of what was happening began to settle in like a heavy fog. The funeral home staff greeted us with professional warmth, yet my mind was elsewhere—still struggling to process that I was walking into this place not for a visit, but for my child's final goodbye. As we entered the main hall where Donovin lay in peaceful repose, the sight of him in the casket almost felt like an out-of-body experience. At first, it didn't seem like him. The child in the soft, blue-and-white casket looked taller, somehow different in appearance than I remembered. But as I got closer, the reality hit me, and I knew—deep in the pit of my stomach—that it was truly him. That brief moment of disbelief gave way to a swell of anger I had been holding in, a sharp, raw pain that pierced my chest. The anger wasn't just directed at the world or at fate—it was directed at God. How could You let this happen? I thought, how could You take him from me?

I couldn't help but ask myself, what kind of God would do this? What kind of love would allow such heartache? A vibrant child, full of life and joy, taken from us too soon— before his first day of kindergarten, before high school, and before all the milestones and memories I had hoped to see him reach. I held it together, though. I had no choice but to push those feelings of anger and betrayal aside, hoping that when the time was right, I would have a private conversation with God about all the questions I was carrying. And, in that moment, I imagined God looking at me with patience, as if to say, I hear you. We'll talk soon.

The funeral service was a blur, a blur of faces, voices, and gestures of sympathy. Yet, amidst the sorrow, I was touched by the sheer number of people who had come to honor my son. People from all walks of life—family, friends, even people who had never met Donovin—gathered in that room to pay their respects. It felt like a sea of faces, all united in grief, and in that sea, I momentarily felt the weight of my loneliness lift. I wasn't alone. Not really. In that space, I could feel the love that surrounded me like a blanket. And though my heart was breaking, it also swelled with gratitude—grateful for how Donovin's light had touched so many lives, even in his brief time here.

The pastor spoke of Donovin's life and of God's love, but I couldn't hear him. Not really. His words felt hollow to me, as if he didn't truly understand the depth of my pain, or the injustice of a young child dying too soon. When he said that Donovin was "back home with the Father," all I could think was, No, God, bring him back home to me. As the pastor continued, I could barely contain my anger, my disbelief. Why had this happened? Why was this the plan?

And then, something unexpected happened—something I had not prepared for, something that left me feeling more fragile than ever. Donovin's father's family, his aunts and uncle, placed a football—a symbol of his father's love—into the casket with Donovin. The sight of it caught me off guard, and a flood of memories from the past year overwhelmed me. I remembered telling Donovin, just a year earlier, that his father had died. He had been so calm, so sure of himself when he reassured me that his father was still watching over him from heaven. How could he have known, at three years old, how to comfort me in the way that he did? How had Donovin grown into such a wise, compassionate little boy?

The sight of the football felt like a subtle reminder that Donovin was never just mine. He belonged to the world in the way only a child can. His capacity for love, for understanding, for offering comfort even in his innocence, was something I could never fully grasp in the moment. As I watched the casket slowly lowered, I fought the impulse to scream, to claw my way out of that reality, but instead, I let my tears fall freely. My heart broke again with every inch of movement, knowing that this was it—this was the final goodbye.

As the service continued, I tried to hold it together, but I couldn't. My grief consumed me. And when the service was over and the guests began to file out, I found myself exhausted—emotionally, physically drained. Most of us returned to my parent's house to continue the tradition of food and fellowship, but it all felt like too much. Too much love, too much sadness, too much to bear. People milled around, chatting and eating, and yet, I just wanted to be alone. Or maybe not alone, but in a space where I could grieve without the eyes of others upon me. My small crew, the people who had been there for me from the start, remained steadfast, surrounding me in a quiet bubble of protection, making sure that I didn't have to face the world alone.

I remember walking into the kitchen, the weight of the day still heavy on my chest, and noticing the spread of food that had been prepared. A mountain of dishes, so much food, it was almost laughable. And yet, I had no appetite. My eyes drifted to the plate in my hand—loaded with food I had no intention of eating. At the top of the pile was a slice of Swiss cheese. I had never liked Swiss cheese. In that moment, I burst out laughing—one of those deep, gut-wrenching laughs that come from somewhere deep inside you when you realize how absurd life has become. My son was gone, and here I was, with a sad piece of cheese on my plate. It felt like a small joke—one that I would probably never get, but I laughed anyway, because sometimes, laughter is the only thing that can get you through the dark.

And then, I thought to myself: maybe this was Donovin's way of sending me one final message. A piece of Swiss cheese, of all things, on the most absurd day of my life. I imagined him, in heaven, laughing right along with me. He had always known how to make me smile, and perhaps, even in death, he was still managing to do the same.

Chapter Eleven

The Struggle to Believe

When my mom told me about meeting a man named R.C. at Walmart who had invited her to his church, I was taken aback. Why was this so-called "Bible thumper" recruiting in a grocery store? Had God really become so desperate for followers that He was sending people to chain stores to find new recruits? Did my mother not realize I was angry with God? Did she not understand that the last thing I wanted to hear about was faith? After all, where was God when I faced heartbreak? Why was He allowing me to suffer? I had so many questions, but the journey to find answers would take months.

Three months after my son Donovin transitioned from this life, I reluctantly agreed to go to a Christian Church in the Phoenix, Arizona Valley, with my mom. From the moment I stepped inside, I was struck by how friendly everyone was. I couldn't shake the feeling that there had to be a catch—surely these nice people were trying to get my money through tithes and offerings. The Pastor stood before the congregation in jeans and a football jersey, sharing stories from his past, including his criminal history. To me, his transparency felt like a ploy to make me trust him. Yet, there was something disarming about him and the Pastor's wife, who was refreshingly relatable and kind.

As I sat through the service, I made it my mission to investigate these people. Surely, this would be a good opportunity to confront God about the pain I was feeling. When I met R.C., the man who had invited my mother, I asked him what R.C. stood for. He smiled and turned the question back on me, which only added to my curiosity. I jokingly responded with "Ridiculously Crazy," and he laughed, revealing his first name was Richard. In that moment, I couldn't help but laugh, surprised by how quickly he had put me at ease.

Despite my skepticism, I continued to meet people at the church, including the Pastor's wife, who greeted me like an old friend. I felt warmth in those interactions, and for a moment, I forgot my reservations. Yet, I reminded myself to stay vigilant; I was still in the midst of my investigation. By the following Sunday, I was eager to hear the next sermon, expecting some slip-up that would confirm my doubts. I was fully engaged, listening intently for anything that felt out of place.

Driving home from that service, I thought about what kind of slip-up I might witness next. Perhaps the pastor would reveal some scandalous behavior or questionable choices. But then, the Pastor spoke candidly about his past struggles with substances and temptation. He didn't glorify those experiences; instead, he emphasized the effort it took to move past them. I was astonished. Here was a man who had faced challenges and yet had chosen to embrace a relationship with God, transforming his life in the process.

It dawned on me that I was witnessing something genuine. The Pastor described his journey as a struggle, one that required constant effort and commitment. The thought that he had truly worked hard to change his life intrigued me. If he could overcome his past and make such a significant shift, perhaps there was hope for me as well. I decided then that I would return for the mid-week service, eager to learn more and curious about the transformative power of faith.

The more I engaged with the church community, the more I began to understand the role of vulnerability and honesty in healing. Each story shared by the pastors and members resonated deeply, shedding light on my own experiences. I started to realize that everyone has their battles and that sharing those struggles can lead to genuine connection, support and renewal.

As the weeks went on, I found myself grappling with my anger toward God. But now, instead of feeling alone, I felt surrounded by a community that accepted me—anger and all. The warmth and understanding I received challenged my previous beliefs about faith and God's presence in my life. Slowly, I began to soften my heart, allowing myself to explore the idea that perhaps there was a way to reconcile my pain with the notion of a loving God, with the notion of cultivating my relationship with God.

In the end, my journey toward faith wasn't a quick fix; it was a gradual unfolding one. It required me to confront my skepticism, to allow myself to feel vulnerable, and to open up to the idea that I could heal, if I truly wanted to heal. Each step I took brought me closer to understanding not just God, but myself. I learned that faith isn't about having all the answers, but about being part of a loving community that supports and uplifts one another, even in the darkest times.

Attending church initially provided me with a sense of community and support that I desperately needed. The warm welcomes and genuine conversations slowly chipped away at the walls I had built around my heart. I found solace in the sermons and connection with others who had faced their own struggles. For a time, the church felt like a safe harbor, a place where I could begin to process my grief and anger. However, as I immersed myself in the experience, I realized that my spiritual journey extended far beyond the walls of that building.

As I became more involved in my own spiritual evolution, I began to understand that while church was a great starting point, it was not the end goal. My relationship with God was meant to be deeply personal, not confined to a Sunday service or a mid-week gathering. I started to seek moments of connection with God outside of church. Whether it was during quiet moments in nature, through journaling my thoughts and prayers, or simply reflecting on life's challenges, I discovered that these personal encounters with God were just as, if not more, profound than anything I experienced within the church community.

I learned that spirituality thrives in everyday moments of life, not just in formal worship settings. This understanding shifted my perspective, leading me to explore various forms of worship—listening to music that resonated with my soul, reading spiritual literature, or even engaging in acts of kindness that felt aligned with my spiritual values. These practices nurtured my connection to God in a way that felt authentic and sustainable. I realized that my relationship with God could flourish outside of structured services and rituals, giving me a sense of freedom and intimacy that I had previously overlooked.

Ultimately, this journey taught me that a genuine relationship with God is built on trust, vulnerability, and the willingness to seek Him in all aspects of life. While the church community had been instrumental in helping me reconnect with my faith, it was the moments of solitude and reflection that truly deepened my understanding of God's love and presence in my life. I now recognize that spirituality is an ongoing journey—one that encourages exploration, questioning, and growth. As I continue to navigate this path, I carry with me the knowledge that God is not confined to a place; He is with me in every moment, guiding me toward a more profound and lasting relationship.

In the months that followed, I came to understand that my anger was not a weakness but a vital part of my healing. Anger had become my armor, protecting me from the vulnerability that I feared would leave me exposed. But as I let myself feel the anger without judgment, I started to see it as a bridge—not to destruction, but to understanding. Anger was a sign that I had deeply loved, and that I had been deeply wounded. It was through confronting that anger, allowing it to rise and fall, that I could begin to ask the harder questions.

One night, during a particularly emotional prayer, I found myself crying out to God in a way I hadn't before. I was still angry, still so sad, but there was something different. It wasn't just a plea for answers; it was a willingness to sit in the pain and trust that God would meet me there. I didn't need to understand everything, but I needed to know that I was not alone. I needed to believe that despite my anger, despite my brokenness, God still saw me and loved me. That night, I felt a sense of peace wash over me—imperfect, fragile peace, but peace nonetheless. It wasn't the resolution I had been expecting, but it was enough to keep me moving forward.

Chapter Twelve

The Depths of Loss

The death of a child is an unbearable experience, one that feels utterly unnatural. As parents, we envision guiding our children through life, expecting that we will eventually pass away after a long, full life, leaving our adult children to continue the cycle. When that expectation is suddenly shattered, whether through a tragic accident or illness, the feelings of loss, fear, anger, disappointment, and betrayal become overwhelming. Haunting questions like *"Why me?"* and *"Why my child?"* emerge. While these questions may never be fully answered by anyone, I learned that God can provide comfort and clarity if we choose to open our hearts and listen—though that is often the hardest part of the journey.

Before discussing how I began to move forward from grief, it's crucial to confront the reality of that pain. The deepest sorrow came from the abrupt end of life as I knew it, a reality I struggled to accept while feeling increasingly guarded against anything related to God. Well-meaning words of condolence from friends, family, and even strangers often felt empty. Unless someone has carried and nurtured a child, held them during their cries, and witnessed their last moments, they cannot fully grasp the profound loss that envelops a grieving parent's soul. Words like *"I'm sorry for your loss"* felt hollow, and I found myself avoiding many people because they couldn't possibly understand the magnitude of what I was going through. In my mind, they were just words, and no one could truly bring Donovin back.

In the days, weeks, and months following my son Donovin's death, I grappled with my emotions. I avoided saying *"Donovin's death"* because it felt too final, opting instead for *"Donovin's transition,"* as I held onto the belief that I would see him again one day. This perspective, however, didn't erase my struggles with sleeping, eating, or even caring for myself. As I continued to maneuver through my grief, there were moments when my mother had to remind me to shower and brush my teeth. Guilt, anger, and a heavy sense of depression consumed me. Even when sleep came, often aided by prescribed medications, I wrestled with the notion that I had no right to rest while grappling with such profound grief. The weight of his absence sat heavily on my chest, as if the air itself had become too thick to breathe.

The darkness of depression felt relentless, gnawing at my soul and mind. I often believed no magic pill could ease the burden of sorrow, and my doctor confirmed that no single medication would erase the pain. While I initially found some relief with a low dose of Prozac, it soon became clear that my underlying despair was far more complex. There were days when I felt so lost that I contemplated ending my own life. Yet, it was during this time of deep struggle that I learned the importance of seeking help, whether through medication or support from loved ones, without shame or stigma. I realized that reaching out wasn't a sign of weakness but a sign of survival, a way of acknowledging that I didn't have to bear this grief alone.

One of the hardest realizations was that grief doesn't wait for you to be ready. It sneaks up on you, waves crashing unexpectedly, sometimes at the most inconvenient moments. I remember standing in the kitchen one day, making a simple meal, when it hit me like a freight train. I had been doing okay for a few hours, my mind occupied with tasks, and then, out of nowhere, the flood gates opened. I collapsed onto the floor, crying uncontrollably. My whole body shook with the force of it, my chest tight with the pain of missing Donovin. It felt like I was being consumed by the grief, as though I would never find my way out of the darkness.

As I navigated this tumultuous journey, I learned that grief has its stages—denial, anger, bargaining, and depression—but these stages do not follow a linear path. My initial denial morphed into intense anger directed at God, questioning why my son was taken from me. I found myself bargaining for a miracle, asking for a sign or a mistake to be revealed. Yet, as I transitioned into deeper layers of depression,

I understood that this was a part of my process, even if it felt insurmountable. I couldn't accept that Donovin was really gone, not because I didn't know it in my mind, but because my heart refused to accept the finality of it. The world felt dimmer without his laughter, quieter without his little voice calling my name.

Ultimately, the journey through grief isn't just about moving forward; it's also about allowing ourselves to feel the full depth of our emotions and acknowledging that healing is a gradual, ongoing process. The darkness of grief cannot be avoided—it must be felt, processed, and eventually released. However, that release often occurs slowly and without a clear timeline. It's essential to remember that God is always present, even in our darkest moments. By embracing both the pain and the hope of eventual healing, we can find a way to honor the memory of our loved ones while also allowing ourselves to keep living. The idea of "moving on" wasn't something I wanted to hear or even consider. To me, "moving on" felt like forgetting. But moving forward—learning how to live without Donovin—was a reality I had to face, no matter how painful.

In time, I began to realize that grief isn't something you "get over." Instead, it becomes a part of you, like a scar that heals over but never quite fades. And through it, I began to discover that, while the path may be fraught with challenges, love and connection endure, guiding us through the shadows toward the light. It is through those moments of connection—whether with family, friends, or even through quiet moments of reflection—that we begin to understand that grief, though powerful, does not define us. The loss of my son will always be a part of me, but it does not have to be all of me.

One of the unexpected gifts of grief, however, was the resilience it uncovered in me. I found strength in the places I never thought to look. With every tear, with every painful step forward, I rediscovered parts of myself that I had forgotten. There were moments when I saw a flicker of joy return, a laugh that caught me by surprise, and even moments of peace amidst the storm. These small glimmers of light were reminders that even in the depths of loss, life still has moments of grace and beauty to offer. Through the messiness of grief, I began to uncover pieces of myself that I hadn't known were there. Resilience. Courage. The ability to keep going, even when every fiber of my being screamed to stop. And in that process, I began to rediscover the capacity for joy, for peace, and for hope.

Grief is not something to conquer—it's something to live with, integrated into the fabric of our being. And as I continue navigating this journey, I hold on to the belief that, though Donovin is no longer with me physically, his spirit still guides me. Through the darkest days, I carry his memory in my heart, and it is through his love that I find the strength to keep moving forward.

Chapter Thirteen

The Weight of Silence

"Mom, did you hear that?" I asked calmly, as I lay on the sofa in the family room of my parents' home in the desert, my mind interpreting the shadow at the kitchen sink as my mother. When she replied, "Hear what?" I knew for certain it was her. I sat up, looked directly at her, and repeated my question as if I hadn't heard her response. "Mom, did you hear that?" Like a looped recording, she echoed, "Hear what?" Panic flooded my mind: Oh no, this is mental illness creeping in; I'm hearing voices.

As I shifted to a fully upright position, I realized how clear and crisp that voice had been, softly speaking only into my right ear. For a moment, I felt a strange relief knowing that the voice I was hearing during my psychosis was gentle, yet masculine, unlike the demonic whispers urging me to harm myself. Or was this just the beginning? Would I end up digesting a full bottle of some random pills and allowing my parents to find me dead? The thought terrified me and simultaneously made me sad, after all, my parents have been through enough grief.

The sound of my father typing away in his distant office interrupted my spiraling thoughts. But my mind snapped back to the voice, refusing to let me ignore it. I felt as if I were a robot responding mechanically: "I understand." Then, I declared to my mother, "I'm going back to work tomorrow!" She looked surprised, questioning me, "Are you sure? You can take your time." I could hear her love and concern, and I felt it deeply. With newfound confidence, I confirmed that I was sure, got up from the sofa, and wandered aimlessly around my parents' desert oasis, convincing myself that I was being productive. Yet, even as I moved through the motions of my day, I felt like I was living in a shell, disconnected from the reality around me.

When I returned to the kitchen, my mother stood in the same spot, now cutting fruit and offering me some. I settled on a cushioned bar stool as she sliced strawberries and green grapes onto a small plate. I fought the urge to refuse them; after all, how could I truly enjoy anything when my son had died? But as the voice echoed in my mind reminding me that I had a choice, I allowed myself to savor the strawberries and grapes, even if the sweetness felt like a betrayal to the grief I carried.

I had been raised as a Christian—well, I attended Sunday School as a child and, as an adult, often only turning to God when I needed something. "Lord, I don't have enough money to pay this bill but thank You for the money I spent having fun at the club." Now, I found myself sitting on that bar stool, confessing as if I were in a confessional with my mom as the priest. I initially hesitated about sharing what the voice had said? Would my mom leave the room to find the number for an urgent psychiatric care facility? Would I scare her? Yet, my mind reminded me that my mom and I had always shared an open and honest relationship. My mom had given birth to me at just 16; we had practically grown up together. She had always been my source of strength and my refuge from the world. Now, she was sharing in my grief and sadness, just as I shared in hers. Before Donovin's death, we could talk about anything, and I questioned why that should change now. Should I call a family meeting, including my dad, to share this revelation? Would sharing what the voice said help them in their own grief? Could I be so selfish as to keep this from them?

My mind was a whirlwind of thoughts, but finally, I blurted out, "He said that I have a choice!" No family meeting was necessary, and if the voice turned out to be a trick, I had now put my mom front and center for what was to come. I felt compelled to clarify what the voice had told me: I could either stay on that sofa and wither away into madness, or I could get up, no matter how painful it was, and take one step forward toward Him. As I spoke, I felt the weight of my confession, unsure of what consequences lay ahead. When I finished, there was a brief silence before my mom responded, joyfully as if she had been waiting for this moment: "Then I stand in agreement with you, but please remember it's okay not to rush yourself." My spirit soared at her words, always recognizing and appreciating her loving support. Her understanding gave me the strength to take that first step, no matter how uncertain it felt.

Back at work on my first day... whose idea was this? I was in Court Management at the time and was unsure of how the drama associated with working in a courthouse would directly affect my new fragile state of mind, and soon, I would realized and witness the power of the God I served.

My supervisor, at the time, was always supportive, but her kindness was especially evident when I returned to the office after Donovin's passing. I noticed the shock on my coworkers' faces as I walked into the employee entrance of the courthouse, even the Judge paused in the hallway upon seeing me; it had only been two months since Donovin left this life. But it was my supervisor's gentle voice immediately saying, "Take your time and do what you need to do for you," that brought me to tears and shattered my defenses. That simple kindness was more than I could handle in that moment. It felt like the world was closing in around me. I had come back to work too soon, and I knew it.

That first day turned out nothing like I had expected. I thought I would dive back into work, but less than 20 minutes in, I found myself back in my car, heading back to my parents' oasis. I was not ready, and my body, my mind, and my soul knew it. The world felt too big, too loud, too harsh. I wasn't ready to face anything beyond the safety of my parents' home. As I drove back to my parents' home, the familiar hum of the car engine guiding me back to my spot on the sofa, provided me some comfort, but it didn't change the aching emptiness in my chest.

On day two, I braced myself for the gentle kindness that would soften my armor and bring me to tears. I made it about 30 minutes before Michael Bublé's "Home" played on the radio—one of Donovin's favorites, played at his funeral. My supervisor and earthly angel came to me and instructed me to go home. Those simple words made me cry all the way to my car. Each time I tried to push myself beyond my limits, my grief reminded me of its power. It was overwhelming, like trying to carry the weight of a thousand pounds on my back, but the pain was relentless. I couldn't pretend to be okay when I wasn't.

Each day, I stayed longer at work, fighting through tears until I no longer rushed back to my parents' house. The training wheels had been removed, and while I knew I had support, I finally felt it was safe to take those steps forward. But then came the realization that I hadn't returned to the home I shared with Donovin. It was time to face that pink elephant in the room. My parents' home was theirs, and it was time to carve out my own space, even if it made me sad to think of living without my son.

Entering our home for the first time since Donovin's death was more traumatic than I had anticipated. I had my support group with my friends and family—but when I stepped into his bathroom and saw his artwork on the walls, I froze. Tears flowed as I erased the removable ink, knowing I wouldn't stay there. I didn't want to erase Donovin, so I took pictures of his art before scrubbing it away. Everywhere I looked, memories of my life with Donovin surrounded me. Hidden toys in my nightstand, hand-drawn pictures in coloring books, and the cheerful message on our answering machine: "We aren't available right now, please leave a message." I didn't want to give away any of his possessions, but the weight of holding onto everything felt overwhelming. Ultimately, I chose to let most of it go, keeping only the items that mattered most—his beloved stuffed animals, drawings, and some favorite toys and clothes.

And there I was again, sitting in our home, slowly sinking back into depression as I recalled every moment we shared. Our first Christmas with our scrawny "Charlie Brown Christmas Tree," which could barely hold decorations. As I cried and packed his belongings, my support group did their best to help, keeping their distance, knowing there was little they could say to ease my sorrow. The silence between us was suffocating, but it was the only thing I could bear.

It would take time to reach the final stage of acceptance. Lying on the soft sofa at my parents' home, I stared at the television, unaware of what was playing. I felt as if I were sinking into a vast pool of Jell-O, hardening around me. I lost all sense of time, and as the shows blended together and the light outside faded, emptiness consumed me. I felt lost in a world of insanity, disinterested in caring for myself. I needed my mother's instructions just to shower, brush my teeth, and change my clothes. Is this how mental illness begins? The question lingered in my mind, but I couldn't find an answer. All I knew was that I was still breathing, even if I didn't know how or why.

Chapter Fourteen

Emerging from the Darkness

As a psychology major, I recognized that I was slipping into depression. I didn't need to consult the *Diagnostic and Statistical Manual of Mental Disorders* (DSM-5) to confirm my feelings, but I didn't fully grasp the severity of my situation at the time. There's something disorienting about mental health struggles—they often don't feel like real, tangible problems. They creep up on you, insidious and slow, until one day you realize you're no longer standing on solid ground. You're sinking into a place of darkness, and you don't even know how you got there.

I thought I had some understanding of grief and pain. After all, I was studying psychology and knew the stages of grief. But nothing could have prepared me for the deep, overwhelming sorrow that enveloped my soul when Donovin passed. In the wake of his death, everything in my life felt unstable, like a puzzle with pieces that no longer fit. The future I had envisioned, one with my child growing up and becoming a part of my life as an adult, vanished in an instant. I felt like I was caught in a whirlwind, spinning uncontrollably, and I had no idea how to stop.

To help manage my depression, I explored various

treatments. While some people are skeptical about medication, I ultimately decided to consult my primary care physician after grappling with multiple dark thoughts, including suicidal ideation. My doctor prescribed an anti-depressant, which I was grateful for, as it helped balance my emotions. The decision to take medication wasn't easy, though. There was part of me that resisted it, not wanting to admit that I couldn't fix myself on my own. But when the weight of sadness felt too much to bear, and I could see no way out of the pit, I chose to accept the help that was offered. What I didn't realize then was that this decision—this act of reaching out for help—was the first thread God was using to weave me into a new understanding of healing.

I found God working in subtle, unexpected ways. Even as I struggled with the darkness that threatened to overtake me, there were moments where I felt a gentle, steady pull—an invitation to continue. The medication was a lifeline, but it was the spiritual renewal, the quiet nudges from God, that truly began to shape my healing. I remember another profound time I felt God's presence in a real way after Donovin's death. It wasn't a dramatic experience. It wasn't a burning bush or an overwhelming rush of emotion. It was just a quiet whisper in my heart, telling me that I was not alone, that He was holding me. He let me know that I had in fact "found" him. It was as if the darkness surrounding me began to tremble at His touch, at His words to me and though the darkness still lingered, it no longer felt as suffocating.

With the personal commitment to myself to not stay on medication for life, I outlined what steps I needed to take to safely come off of medication and find a holistic alternative.

First, I needed to get my emotional well-being on track, to stabilize enough so I could begin addressing the deeper causes of my pain. As I navigated this journey, I also turned to natural remedies, something that felt more in line with my sense of control. As a tea enthusiast, I focused on herbal teas, convinced that they could offer some relief. I scoured countless articles and even consulted with herbalists, discovering options like chamomile, St. John's Wort, and valerian root—each with its own calming properties. I compiled a small list of herbs that I found promising, hoping that they would provide a soothing balm for my troubled mind. But, much like my journey with medication, I began to see that these small acts of self-care were not just ways to ease my pain—they were ways God was working through me, teaching me how to care for myself in a new, gentler way.

Along the way, I learned to celebrate my memories without allowing them to hinder my growth. This was not an easy process; it required difficult, moment-by-moment conversations with myself and with God. Some of these conversations were painful and brought up feelings of anger, resentment, and self-pity, leaving me in tears on my bed or the floor. The emotional struggle was draining, but I was determined to emerge from the darkness stronger, after all, Donovin was watching. At times, it felt like I could physically see the darkness around me, taunting me and telling me that I had every right to wallow in my negative emotions and self-destructive behaviors. Yet, amid that darkness, I felt God's quiet encouragement to stand back up, to live, and to love again. I realized that this pain, this heartbreak, was not the end of my story but a chapter in a much larger narrative that God was still writing. The threads of my pain, my anger, my sorrow, were being woven together into something beautiful, something I couldn't yet fully comprehend.

Life is a deeply personal journey, and we all have the potential to navigate it healthily, wisely, and prosperously if we choose to turn away from darkness. Remember that you can endure the hard times and celebrate the good ones, if we choose to.

One of the most profound lessons I've learned is that life does not unfold in a linear fashion. We have moments of overwhelming joy, followed by moments of intense pain. Yet, if we can find the strength to move through the pain, we create space for joy to return. Healing is not a one-time event—it is a continuous process. Each day spent finding balance, each step toward emotional recovery brings us closer to a place where light can break through the shadows. I slowly began to understand that healing wasn't about erasing the pain or forgetting Donovin. It was about accepting the pain, not as something to be endured, but as a part of the journey. In this acceptance, a quiet peace emerged, one that didn't rely on the absence of pain but on the ability to coexist with it.=It was about being honest with myself about my feelings. It was about cultivating my personal relationship with God.

The journey of faith often reveals a profound truth: God is not lost; we are. In times of struggle and confusion, it's easy to feel distant from the divine. We may grapple with doubts or succumb to the pressures of life, thinking that we have drifted away from God. Yet, the reality is that God remains steadfast, always ready to welcome us back into a loving relationship. It's in our moments of feeling lost that we can truly begin to understand the nature of God—not as an abstract concept tied to rituals, but as a deeply personal presence that yearns for connection. This realization shifted my perspective on faith. I began to see life not as a list of obligations, but as an invitation to experience God in the depths of my sorrow and in the quiet moments of my recovery.

Believing that God allows pain not as punishment, but as a means to bring us closer to Him, can be a difficult truth to accept. In moments of suffering, it's easy to feel abandoned or question why a loving God would permit such hardship. The idea that pain serves a higher purpose—one that ultimately brings us into a deeper relationship with Him—can feel like an emotional paradox.

We yearn for comfort and relief, yet the thought that growth often comes through the crucible of pain forces us to confront our own vulnerability and trust in a divine plan that we may not fully understand. It's a challenging pill to swallow because it asks us to embrace suffering not as a sign of God's absence, but as a pathway to greater closeness with Him.

Religion, with its rituals and regulations, can sometimes create a barrier between us and God. We may find ourselves caught up in the expectations and traditions of organized faith, losing sight of the personal relationship that God desires with each of us. This can lead to a sense of obligation rather than genuine connection. When we shift our focus from religious practices to building a relationship, we open ourselves to experiencing God's love in a transformative way. It is in these moments of authenticity that we discover a deeper sense of belonging and purpose. For me, the turning point came when I allowed myself to see God as someone who was walking beside me—not a distant judge, but a companion through my pain. I began to find a God who wasn't just a deity to be worshipped, but a Father who was intimately involved in my journey, loving me through the sorrow and comforting me in my deepest pain.

To cultivate this relationship, we must engage in honest conversations with ourselves and with God, expressing our fears, hopes, sadness, confusion, loneliness, anger, and desires. Prayer becomes more than a routine; it evolves into a dialogue where we can share our struggles and seek guidance on a daily basis. This intimate communication helps us to reconnect and realign ourselves with God's presence in our lives and His ultimate purpose for our lives. Rather than viewing prayer as a task, we can see it as a lifeline, a way to navigate through the complexities of life while feeling anchored in divine love. There were moments when I felt utterly lost, but prayer became my tether, reminding me that I was not alone, even when I couldn't sense God's presence in any tangible way.

As we foster this relationship, we begin to recognize that God is always present, even in our darkest moments. When we feel lost, we can look for the signs of God's presence around us—in nature, in the kindness of others, and in those quiet moments of reflection. These experiences remind us that God is not waiting for us to follow a set of rules; instead, God invites us to embrace the fullness of life with an open heart. It is through this lens that we find clarity and direction. This realization did not come easily. I had to let go of my own expectations and trust that God's presence was not bound by my understanding or my timeline. I began to see that each painful step, each tear shed, was part of God's healing process. The veil of darkness began to lift, not because I had overcome my grief, but because I had learned to lean into it, trusting that God was with me every step of the way.

Ultimately, understanding that we are the ones who can lose our way, rather than God, empowers us to seek a deeper connection. By prioritizing relationship over religion, we can navigate our spiritual journeys with grace and authenticity. God's love is ever-present, ready to guide us home, encouraging us to lean into that relationship and find our way back to a place of peace and understanding. It was in this quiet surrender, where I no longer relied on my own strength alone, that I began to find the light—slowly at first, like the first rays of dawn piercing the night sky but gradually growing stronger.

God allowed me to be woven in the wake of grief, where I found the strength to move forward, not because I was strong enough on my own, but because I had learned to rely on God's steady presence, His quiet whispers of comfort, and the deep assurance that even in my brokenness, I was being held, reshaped, and carried toward a place of healing.

Donovin Malachi Stokes

Resources

Free Grief & Mindset Digital Resources

https://www.stan.store/FrankieKounouho

Find a therapist

Psychology Today

https://www.therapists.psychologytoday.com

GoodTherapy.org

https://www.goodtherapy.org - 1-888-563-2112

National Institute of Mental Health

https://www.nimh.nih.gov/health/topics/depression
1-866-615-6464 (toll-free)
1-301-443-8431 (TTY)
1-866-415-8051 (TTY toll-free)
Available in English and Spanish
Monday through Friday - 8:30 a.m. to 5:00 p.m. ET

Suicide Prevention Helplines

Suicide Hotline: 1-800-SUICIDE (2433) – Can use in US, U.K., Canada, and Singapore

Suicide Crisis Line: 1-800-999-9999

National Suicide Prevention Helpline: 1-800-273-TALK (8255)

National Adolescent Suicide Helpline: 1-800-621-4000

Suicide & Depression Crisis Line – Covenant House: 1-800-999-9999

Depression Helplines

Postpartum Depression: 1-800-PPD-MOMS

NDMDA Depression Hotline: Support Group: 1-800-826-3632

Additional Resources

Veterans: 1-877-VET2VET

Crisis Help Line – For Any Kind of Crisis: 1-800-233-4357

Befrienders Worldwide: http://www.befrienders.org/

Mental Health America

The leading community-based non-profit network in the United States, supplying resources for living a mentally healthy life.

mentalhealthamerica.net or call 1-800-969-6642

National Alliance on Mental Illness (NAMI)

This is the nation's largest grassroots mental health organization.

nami.org or call 1-800-950-6264

National Council for Behavioral Health (National Council)

The National Council is the unifying voice of America's community mental health and addictions treatment organizations.

thenationalcouncil.org or call 1-202-684-7457

Disclaimer

Please note that while the resources listed are provided for informational purposes, this does not constitute an endorsement or guarantee of the services offered by any of the entities mentioned. Users are encouraged to conduct their own research and exercise discretion when utilizing these resources.

For information on grief or mindset coaching, please contact us.

Frankie Kounouho, MCPC, CLC
E-mail us at: info@mbtcoaching.org
Instagram: @2bfrankiek

Content Disclaimer

The information in this book was compiled from various sources and personal experiences by the Author. Individuals are encouraged to seek professional counsel in determining their need for psychiatric or mental health assessment.

All information and resources provided in this book are provided for information purposes only and does not constitute a legal contract or other covenant, endorsement, or agreement of any kind. Although the information and resources found in this book is believed to be reliable, no warranty, expressed or implied, is made regarding the accuracy, adequacy, completeness, legality, reliability, or usefulness of any information or resource, either isolated or in the aggregate.

This book and its author (i) are not liable for any improper or incorrect use of the information or resources in this book, (ii) assume no responsibility for anyone's use of or reliance on any such information, (iii) are not liable for any damages (of any type, for any reason, however caused, or under any theory of liability) arising in any way out of the use of the information or resources in this book, even if advised of the possibility of that damage.

References

American Psychiatric Association. (2013). *Diagnostic and statistical manual of mental disorders* (5th ed.). Arlington, VA: American Psychiatric Association.

Beck, A. T., Brown, G. B., & Steer, R. A. (1996). *Manual for the Beck Depression Inventory-II (BDI-II)*. San Antonio, TX: The Psychological Corporation.

Bible Gateway. (n.d.). *Bible Gateway online resource*. Retrieved June 1, 2017, from https://www.biblegateway.com

Google.com (2018, July 10). *What are monsoons?* Retrieved from https://www.google.com online definitions from Oxford Languages.

Ippen, C. G., & Wong, C. (2005). *Beck Depression Inventory-Second Edition (BDI-II)*. NCTSN Measure Review Database. National Child Traumatic Stress Network. Retrieved from https://www.nctsn.org

Open Bible. (n.d.). *Open Bible online resource*. Retrieved June 1, 2017, from http://www.openbible.com

www.ingramcontent.com/pod-product-compliance
Lightning Source LLC
Chambersburg PA
CBHW050008100426
42739CB00011B/2557